SIMPLE ACTS

Pau-

Thank you for Housing

The vision and space for the

Hudson Institute. I'm so much

better for it and this book

became possible because

of it. All good

things.

Jason

9/14/20

SIMPLE ACTS

PRACTICES FOR A BROKEN WORLD

JASON L KESSLER

NEW DEGREE PRESS

SIMPLE ACTS
Practices for a Broken World

ISBN   978-1-64137-938-0   *Paperback*
          978-1-64137-740-9   *Kindle Ebook*
          978-1-64137-741-6   *Ebook*

To all the potential and possibility for good...

McNamara iPhone photo, Johns Island, SC, December 28, 2018.

CONTENTS

———

INTRODUCTION   9

SECTION ONE   **19**
CHAPTER ONE   FOR THE SAKE OF WHAT   21
CHAPTER TWO   HOW WE GOT HERE   33
CHAPTER THREE   THE LIZARD BRAIN?   47

SECTION TWO   **61**
CHAPTER FOUR   THE POWER OF NOW   63
CHAPTER FIVE   WHERE IS YOUR BREATH?   73
CHAPTER SIX   TRY LISTENING FOR A CHANGE   87
CHAPTER SEVEN   CHEW YOUR FOOD   97
CHAPTER EIGHT   WALKING   105
CHAPTER NINE   I SMELL THAT   115

SECTION THREE   **125**
CHAPTER TEN   INFORMAL PRACTICE   127
CHAPTER ELEWEN   THE OVERVIEW EFFECT   137
CHAPTER TWELVE   ONGOING PRACTICE   149

                   ACKNOWLEDGMENTS   161
                   APPENDIX   163

INTRODUCTION

———

By the time you finish this sentence, time has changed. Not only the clock changed, even by just seconds, but your experience has changed. You are now different for having read that sentence. Maybe you notice an itch on your nose or a grumble in your stomach. That sentence may have sparked a memory from the past or launched a vision of the future. These small, seemingly insignificant examples of changes in your experience repeat continually every moment of every day and eventually add up to more measurable, observable changes. We don't typically notice these momentary changes, but we do notice when a day, a year, or even a lifetime has passed and we look back, reflecting on the changes. All we need to do is to wait long enough, and eventually we will recognize the change. That experience of daily, yearly, or lifetime change is an accumulation of momentary changes.

Here is a practice to measure daily change. Take out your trusty phone with that fancy camera, note the time, and take a photograph of something in the natural world that interests or inspires you. Many of us will choose ourselves, which is fine, and noting the time is important, but also note the framing of the photograph because you need to take the same photo at the same time the next day. Once you've captured that second photograph, compare the two and take some time to observe the differences between them. I guarantee they will not be identical.

While our experience of momentary change is fleeting and oftentimes not very impactful, the world we've created for ourselves is more connected to others and things outside of our direct experience, so it can feel incredibly overwhelming. Our modern world, connected by the internet, cannot only bring our geographically dispersed loved ones into our daily experience or teachings and trainings from across the globe into everyday learning, but also bring the suffering, pain, and misery of all kinds of living creatures directly into our hearts. For all the good our modern, connected world provides, it can also bring with it increased anxiety and suffering. We are exposed to so many things that seem out of our control and not in our direct experience that it can be overwhelming.

In April 2019, the American Psychiatric Association (APA) conducted a poll and found that "about two in three Americans say they are extremely or somewhat anxious about keeping themselves and their family safe, paying bills and their health....Nearly one in three adults (32 percent) say they are more anxious than they were last year; more than four in ten (43 percent) say they are about as anxious as they were last year; and about a quarter (24 percent) say they are less anxious than last year. These are similar to changes in anxiety reported over the last two years."[1]

---

[1] "Americans' Overall Level of Anxiety about Health, Safety and Finances Remain High," APA News Release, American Psychiatric Association, accessed April 10, 2020.

People are clearly suffering. And this data is just for the United States, population 329,500,934 as of April 10, 2020, at 3:25 p.m. EDT. Expand that to the globe, population 7,642,269,682 as of April 10, 2020, at 3:26 p.m. EDT, and we are talking about a lot of suffering.[2] When I look around the world, I see a tremendous number of systems that are broken and contributing to this suffering. These are systems we humans have designed, yet they are not serving us, or at least not all of us. Let's just look at food.

In 2018, "11.1 percent of US households were food insecure at least some time during the year, including 4.3 percent with very low food security, where the food intake of one or more household members was reduced and their eating patterns disrupted at times because the household lacked money and other resources for obtaining food."[3]

Yet the USDA's (United States Department of Agriculture) Economic Research Service estimates "31 percent food loss at the retail and consumer levels, corresponded to approximately 133 billion pounds and $161 billion worth of food in 2010."[4]

When so many people are going hungry and we are throwing food away, the system is clearly broken and needs to change.

Yet like all the broken, incomplete, and inefficient systems we have constructed, these systems are made up of people. Human

---

2   "U.S. and World Population Clock," U.S. Census Bureau, accessed April 10, 2020.

3   Alisha Coleman-Jensen, "Household Food Security in the United States in 2018," U.S. Department of Agriculture, Economic Research Service, *Economic Research Report* Number 270 (September 2019): Abstract.

4   "Why should we care about food waste?" USDA, accessed April 10, 2020.

beings. Us. I believe if we want to transform the broken systems in the world, we must begin by transforming ourselves.

As a certified executive coach, I focus on supporting people to transform their lives, and for me that means getting people "into their bodies." For most, the idea of getting into their body is a foreign concept, and that is part of the problem right there. People **think** about it as a concept. I push them to **experience** it as sensation and feeling. People commonly identify or **think** of themselves as their thoughts, disconnected from the sensations they feel. I invite people "into their bodies" to feel sensation. Since our bodies are our first and fundamental "home," I have always felt they are where our self-work needs to begin.

Unfortunately, for many people, the body is a painful place. Dealing with trauma or associations of shame makes even the thought of getting "into the body" really scary. Sadly, this fear is another example of the systemic issues we have created through which society can tell people their body is wrong or bad. I offer these simple acts as a new way to feel about your body. Do as much as feels comfortable and know that one of my goals is to get people beyond judgment and into feeling, but this work can be tough. Move at your own pace and in a way that feels safe to you.

My own work in the world has cycled from working with individuals as a teacher or coach to working on large-scale global problems like planetary defense from asteroids. While I have had the distinct privilege to serve the country at one of the greatest organizations in the world, NASA (National Aeronautics and Space Administration), I have learned that as overwhelming as problems may feel, they can be broken down into simple steps. So to support change and transformation, this book is about the simple acts we can take to create change in ourselves and thereby change in the local, national, and global problems we face.

This complex world we have created for ourselves is filled with systemic challenges that already negatively affect our lives. We can proactively engage in the redesign of these systems or continue to suffer the consequences. To best support ourselves in the work necessary to make the changes needed, we must move quickly. It can be easy for me to get stuck and overwhelmed by how big the challenges are and how powerless I am. This stagnation happens when I think about the people going hungry as food gets wasted and trucked to our landfills. While this book is about change and the simple acts we can take, it is also ultimately about empowerment, because that is what people need right now.

When I do feel overwhelmed, I take a moment to reflect on simple acts and the power of one individual. Greta Thunberg is the perfect example. In August 2018, at fifteen years old, the Swede decided to skip school and hold a sign up outside of the Swedish parliament that read, "School Strike for Climate." That simple act sparked a global movement. Thunberg addressed the United Nations and World Economic Forum multiple times and was selected as *Time Magazine*'s Person of the Year in 2019, the youngest recipient in history.

Simple does not mean easy. It was not easy to face the ridicule, attacks, or demonization. But simple acts can compound into great change. We **need** to sweat the small stuff. This book is based on my own journey, which is ongoing, but starts within my body. Every action we make or take starts within our bodies as we make a decision that is accomplished by moving our bodies. Or not moving our bodies, like Greta standing outside of parliament.

These simple acts we will explore start with things we do or can do in our bodies. Every day. Many times per day. Becoming conscious and aware of my body and noticing what is happening within it brings me into the present moment, and possibility springs from the present moment. The gift of these simple acts is when done consciously, they can lead to empowerment through the options of possibility.

I wrote this book for anyone who is looking for some simple things they can do to transform their lives. I have been successful coaching folks who were looking to shift into more fulfilling work opportunities by either stepping into new roles within their existing workplace or moving to new organizations for more responsibilities. Through the process of working with these folks, I have come to realize that at its core, even though they didn't always realize it at the time, the practice of simple acts was foundational to their transformation.

Whether you are an executive looking to level up your skills, middle management looking to increase your capacity to make bigger offers, navigating your first job or challenges at school of any level, wanting to get involved in your community, any family member looking to shift their family dynamic, and certainly anyone who wants to create change in the world to address the kinds of large-scale threats humanity faces, these simple acts can help.

I started writing this book before the COVID-19 pandemic, but our new reality makes these simple acts feel even more relevant, necessary, and important. Because we are all navigating a new normal in our lives, I try to keep this book simple. You'll get material about the increased complexity and stress we are feeling in the world today supported by data and science. Most importantly, you'll get simple practices you can do every day to help support your efforts to consciously change yourself and the world.

This book will be grounded in science and research, and it is designed for you to jump around and choose what is most interesting to you. While the book has been organized like a vinyl album designed to be experienced in a certain way, I encourage you to explore what works for you. Most importantly, it is a simple invitation back "home" and into feeling the sensations in your body.

Before we begin this conversation—and yes, this really is a conversation—the first thing I ask you do is to reflect on how and why you came to be reading this book. Maybe someone gave it to you. Maybe you liked the cover artwork. Maybe you consciously sought it out. No matter the reason, just take a moment to reflect on it. And another moment.

Now think about why you might want to read it. Continuing to read is a choice, and while I do consider this book a conversation, I've already made my choice to be in it.

If you are seriously considering the choice to continue reading, then please get clear on intention, or what we'll call "for the sake of what" you are reading this book. The answer to this question will likely change, but it will also sustain you in the process. This intention is a choice you will need to make repeatedly if you are going to finish this book. It is an incredibly important question to get in the practice of asking yourself. It helps bring clarity to our motivations. As Simon Sinek brilliantly reminded us in his famous TED Talk, "Start with the Why."[5]

Before we get started, I want to introduce myself. I'm a white, married, heterosexual, nondisabled cis male, raised in the suburbs outside of New York City with lots of time spent with my grandparents in their small town (population 1,391) in Arkansas. I thought of myself as upper middle class, but really it was an upper-class experience. I grew up Jewish, and my momma had converted from Episcopalian, so I had Christian and Jewish parents. I also had both perceived and unperceived privilege, lots of love, and a belief anything was possible. The oldest of two boys, I have been to every state in the United States, lived in eight of them, and traveled to thirty countries around the world, often for work.

All of these things have formed my experience. Yet as I explore what it means to be all of those identities, I struggle with understanding the experience of others—racism and white fragility, sexism, homophobia, transphobia, xenophobia, religious persecution, classism. I return home to

---

5   *TED*, "Simon Sinek: How Great Leaders Inspire Action," March 10, 2014,
     Video, 17:58.

my body to help navigate through the cauldron of emotion those experiences create for me and notice what they feel like and where I'm feeling them. I hope this book provides you some understanding and practice to help support you in the transformation you seek.

SECTION ONE

CHAPTER ONE

FOR THE SAKE OF WHAT

———

I had the privilege of working at NASA for nearly fifteen years. I attended over twenty space shuttle launches, visited every NASA center, and got to know and work with brilliant people from across the agency. The work is diverse—from research on improving aircraft safety to measuring our changing planet and exploring the origins of the universe, to what everyone associates with NASA: landing humans on the moon. The space agency is the pinnacle of human intellectual accomplishment.

For some of my time at NASA, I directly supported Dan Goldin, the longest-serving NASA administrator, as his executive assistant. This job meant I attended his meetings, ensured he had all his background material for meetings and attempted to keep him on schedule, and when traveling, ensured we got wherever we needed to be next.

It was truly the world's greatest classroom, taking me all over the world for conversations about the ultimate in human exploration. I witnessed the management of the world's premier space agency and learned about the search for life on Mars, the discovery of a method to find planets around other stars, and the ability of satellite measurements to track changes on the surface of the earth. I listened to the astronauts share their excitement about their upcoming space shuttle missions and sometimes got to greet them upon their return to Florida. It was beyond my wildest dream job. Plus, Dan really took me under his wing and helped me grow exponentially in my twenties. I am forever grateful.

Among the many things I learned during my time at NASA, which I wasn't expecting, was my tendency to be "in my head" or "stuck in my head." It is no surprise, as the work is just so heady. My NASA experience helped launch me onto my journey of self-discovery, into my body and the simple acts I'm sharing in this book.

Let's take a quick step back. This idea of getting into one's body is likely very foreign. I have had a number of teachers use this quote from James Joyce's The Dubliners: "Mr. Duffy lived a short distance from his body." It is an amazing quote because it captures the concept of being in one's head, not in one's body. That short distance is often the thoughts in our brain, and the body is often taken for granted as the locomotion that moves our head or "us" around.

As we have moved into a knowledge economy in which so much value is created by our minds and not our bodies, we often identify even less with our bodies. Of course, there are times at the gym doing the obligatory exercise when we can feel our bodies as we push our limits, but how often is that gym time spent somewhere else? Either watching TV, reading a magazine, or listening to music or a podcast. Even manual labor is often done without being fully present in the body. Folks are thinking about the past or dreaming about the future or simply anticipating when work will be over.

We are going to take time in this book to consciously get "into our bodies," feeling sensation. This idea is empowering because our bodies manifest action in the world. Our brain may think it up, but it is often our bodies that make it happen. I will be offering a series of practices you can use to feel into your body. These practices will also be about accessing the present moment.

Through our bodies, we will step into the present moment. It is a powerful place, your body in the moment, because it is a place full of possibilities, and therefore choice. When you are in the present moment and in your body, you are creating the future. Often we forget we are always in our bodies in the present moment when we are frequently distracted in our minds reflecting on the past or dreaming about the future.

"For the sake of what?" This question is such a powerful place to start because it can clarify and illuminate why you are doing something. While I don't always consider this question as I'm making a multitude of choices, I do check in with it for the important stuff. I'm going to ask you throughout this book to come back to this question: "for the sake of what?"

Let's step back even further. It is May 25, 1961, and President John F. Kennedy is addressing Congress about urgent national needs:

"First, I believe that this nation should commit itself to achieving the goal, before this decade is out, of landing a man on the moon and returning him safely to the earth. No single space project in this period will be more impressive to mankind, or more important for the long-range exploration of space; and none will be so difficult or expensive to accomplish."[6]

For context, on April 12, 1961, just over a month earlier, the Soviet Union had once again beaten the United States in the space race by launching Yuri Gagarin into space, where he orbited the earth one time before returning home safely. What I find fascinating is that Kennedy did not really like space much before he was president.

As a US senator from Massachusetts from 1953 to 1960, Kennedy had displayed a marked lack of interest in space. Aerospace pioneer Charles Draper of the Massachusetts Institute of Technology (MIT) remembered when, a few years before the 1960 election, he met Kennedy and his brother Robert at a Boston restaurant, hoping to get them interested in space exploration. The Kennedy brothers, said Draper, treated his pitch with good-natured ridicule. According to Draper, JFK and RFK "could not be convinced that all rockets were not a waste of money and space navigation even worse."[7]

---

6   President John F. Kennedy, "Special Message by the President on Urgent National Needs," Address to Congress, May 25, 1961.

7   Richard E. Collin, "'We Choose to Go to the Moon', JFK and the Race for the Moon, 1960-1963" in John F. Kennedy History, Memory, Legacy: An Interdisciplinary Inquiry, ed. John Delane Williams, Robert G. Waite and Gregory S Gordon (University of North Dakota, UND Scholarly Commons), 167-68.

Yet Kennedy found himself in new circumstances as president, and Gagarin's successful spaceflight changed everything.

JFK told NASA administrator James Webb that a moon landing goal was risky, since failure would be embarrassing. Webb responded that exploring space wasn't just about a timeline; there were scientific and technological advantages involved. JFK disagreed. "This is, whether we like it or not, a race," he said. "Everything we do [in space] ought to be tied into getting to the moon ahead of the Russians...otherwise we shouldn't be spending this kind of money, because I'm not that interested in space."[8]

Jerome Wiesner, the president's science adviser, "had argued against a lunar landing, advocating instead a scientifically justifiable program. He recommended a water desalination project or even a program to provide more food for the poor, but he eventually realized that he was fighting a losing battle since it was 'a political, not a technical issue.'"[9]

It is very easy for those of us born after July 20, 1969, the day of the Apollo 11 moon landing, to only see the accomplishment and human triumph and forget the commitments necessary to overcome the social, political, technical, and financial challenges the space program faced in its early days. It was Kennedy's transformation and commitment to beating the Soviets in the space race in those early days that led to the American flag being planted on the surface of the moon

8   Editors of LIFE, "LIFE John F. Kennedy: The Legacy a 100-Year Commemorative Edition," *LIFE*, May 29, 2017.

9   Derek W. Elliot, "Space: The Final Frontier of the New Frontier" in Kennedy: The New Frontier Revisited, ed. Mark J. White (NYU Press, 1998), 200.

that summer day in 1969. While he didn't live to see the accomplishment, Kennedy had answered the question "for the sake of what?"

So I offer up this inquiry—"for the sake of what?"—as a new practice. This book is going to be full of practices you can adopt, and I believe it is important to consider your motivation as a first practice. Now, practice may be a scary word. It can be for me. So let's unpack it a bit. According to Oxford, a practice is:

1. The actual application or use of an idea, belief, or method, as opposed to theories relating to it.
2. The customary, habitual, or expected procedure or way of doing something.
3. Repeated exercise in or performance of an activity or skill so as to acquire or maintain proficiency in it.[10]

I'm hoping we can start with definition number one and move from theory into the application of these ideas. With time, we can hope to graduate to definition number three as we acquire and maintain our proficiency.

As a beginning practice, I invite you to take a moment and explore "for the sake of what" you might be reading this book. There are countless other things you could be doing with your time right now. Reading this book is a choice. I encourage you to set it down or stop the audio and take a moment to consider this question: "for the sake of what are you reading this book right now?"

---

10   *Lexico powered by Oxford,* s.v. "practice (n.)," accessed April 19, 2020.

If you are like me, you likely took a momentary pause but continued right to this sentence. I get it, this question is hard, and we're not used to asking it. My request is that you at least hold this question in the back of your mind, something there to consider and continually explore and come back to, both for reading this book and for other actions you take that have meaning.

For me, the seed of this book came out of a conversation with my good friend Jeremiah. We were in one of our coach trading sessions in which we take turns receiving and practicing coaching at the same time. We schedule an hour together, and for approximately the first thirty minutes, one of us is the coach and the other a client, and then we switch roles for the rest of our scheduled time. It has proven so valuable because we take the time to provide feedback on the coaching we have received. The feedback is well grounded in direct experience and explained well by a client who is also a coach, and the coach can explain some of the choices made. It is such a gift to have this kind of relationship, and I know it makes me a better coach.

Do you have a confidant you can trust to provide honest feedback about how you are showing up in the world? Do you even want to know?

Jeremiah is a voracious reader and seems to always be into the next book exploring some aspect of coaching or leadership, and he was in the midst of a new one exploring attention and awareness. Jeremiah had started a new practice of using his eyes to focus on different things. This simple practice of focusing his eyes narrowly on the words on his computer screen in an email he was writing and then shifting his focus to a more diffused awareness of his surroundings in his office radically shifted his experience and he was buzzing about it. His energy proved contagious and set me on the path to writing this book.

I can remember getting up during that call and pacing with enthusiasm as I felt his energy. I showed up to that call reflecting broadly on the challenges the world seemed to be facing and thinking about how to create a good offer to support people interested in transforming the world and the broken systems that maintain social and economic inequalities, fossil fuel dependence, and limited access to healthcare and education. We roughly sketched out an approach for a series of workshops designed for an experience to aid in that transformation.

I became focused on the experience to support transformation and found this definition of experience perfect:

> *the sense of something you personally accomplish, something that you do to affect outcomes, or something that makes you feel a certain way (e.g., I had a great time playing tennis).*[11]

Over the next month and a half, I played with this idea of designing an experience to support transformation and then

---

11   J. Robert Rossman and Mathew D. Duerden, *Designing Experiences,* (Columbia University Press, 2019), Chapter One.

happily found the support I needed to write the book I hadn't realized I needed to write. It started out with this broad goal of transformation, but it wasn't until I refined my "for the sake of what" into the simple acts we all make that it could be the foundation for personal transformation. Through personal transformation, we can change the broken systems of which we all are part.

So my "for the sake of what" of this book is to support personal transformation so you can become more empowered and present in the moment and thereby be able to see and make new choices.

In case you are having a hard time choosing a reason to keep reading, I want to offer my favorite poem of all time. I offer it to you now as you think about "for the sake of what" should you choose to continue reading.

The Journey
By Mary Oliver

One day you finally knew
what you had to do, and began,
though the voices around you
kept shouting
their bad advice—
though the whole house
began to tremble
and you felt the old tug
at your ankles.

"Mend my life!"
each voice cried.
But you didn't stop.
You knew what you had to do,
though the wind pried
with its stiff fingers
at the very foundations,
though their melancholy
was terrible.
It was already late
enough, and a wild night,
and the road full of fallen
branches and stones.
But little by little,
as you left their voices behind,
the stars began to burn
through the sheets of clouds,
and there was a new voice
which you slowly
recognized as your own,
that kept you company
as you strode deeper and deeper
into the world,
determined to do
the only thing you could do —
determined to save
the only life you could save.[12]

12   Mary Oliver, "The Journey" in *Dream Work, (New York: The Atlantic Monthly Press, 1986*

For your next practice, I encourage you to read this poem to someone you care about and then have them read it back to you. I suggest you find the time to experience the words as a recipient and as a giver. See what happens.

When you hear the words read back to you, does your experience of the meaning change? When you read the words to someone else, does your experience of the meaning change? This practice is the beginning of bringing awareness to your own experience and how interacting with others changes it.

I request you withhold judgement about the experience and simply notice. I should have warned you earlier that you will likely make some assessment or have a tendency to want to assess the experience, and your assessment is not what I'm hoping to explore with you. I'm here to explore the experience as simply as possible.

The book is broken into three sections, and you are invited to jump between sections and chapters and even skip anything that doesn't resonate. I find rereading a book or text that taught me something or made me feel a certain way at one time and upon rereading, sometimes many years later, finding completely new things and feeling differently about it to be a cool experience. Since this book is an asymmetric conversation, follow your own path.

The first section attempts to set some context and foundation for my sense of the state of the world. The second section lays out the practices of the simple mindset. The third section is designed to help you take the practices out into the world.

Thanks for sticking with me so far and joining me on a journey into your own awareness.

CHAPTER SUMMARY

Often taken for granted, we are going to focus on **feeling our body** as we explore experiences in new ways. For us, experience is going to mean *the sense of something you personally accomplish, something you do to affect outcomes*, or *something that makes you feel a certain way*. The simple acts within this book are invitations into your body, and the associated practices will support you with new ways to consider this primal relationship. For us, practice is going to mean **"the actual application or use of an idea, belief, or method, as opposed to theories relating to it."**

Before we focus on feeling the body, though, our first step is to explore our motivations. Understanding these motivations will help support us as we make commitments to practice. To help with this exploration, we are going to use the question **"for the sake of what?"** as a new practice.

CHAPTER TWO

HOW WE GOT HERE

___

My grandpa, Hugh Wilson Blevins, was born in Dardanelle, Arkansas in 1920. Smack dab in the middle of what Robert J. Gordon calls "the special century" in his excellent book *The Rise and Fall of American Growth*.[13] For Gordon, the special century measures from 1870 to 1970; a flash in the history of humanity.

> *Modern humans first emerged about 100,000 years ago. For the next 99,800 years or so, nothing happened. Well, not quite nothing. There were wars, political intrigue, the invention of agriculture—but none of that stuff had much effect on the quality of people's lives. Almost everyone lived on the modern equivalent of $400 to $600 a year, just above subsistence level. True there were always tiny aristocracies who lived far better, but numerically they were quite insignificant. Then—just a couple of hundred years ago—people started getting richer. And richer and richer still.*[14]

---

13 Robert J. Gordon, *The Rise and Fall of American Growth*, (Princeton: Princeton University Press, 2016) Page 1.

14 Steven Landsberg, "A Brief History of Economic Time," *The Wall Street Journal,* June 9, 2007.

Oxford describes quality of life as "the standard of health, comfort, and happiness experienced by an individual or group,"[15] and my grandpa was born at the leading edge of the exponential improvement in humanity's standard. This time would be the most radical transformation of our planet since a meteor struck Earth just off the Northern coast of Mexico's Yucatán Peninsula just about sixty-six million years ago. Sourcing relevant and trusted data, Gordon's book focuses on the United States and describes how back in 1870, a US household could be considered completely isolated by modern standards, and by 1940, only seventy years later, it could be connected in five different ways with electricity, gas, telephone, running water, and waste disposal.

Take a moment for that to sink into your body. One of the things I love about my wife is her perspective and appreciation. She loves to take a hot bath, and nearly every time she does, she expresses gratitude for the on-demand hot, running water piped into her tub. Gordon shares this historical fact in his TED Talk: "In 1885, the average North Carolina housewife walked 148 miles a year carrying thirty-five tons of water."[16]

Let that one sink into your body—maybe a little bit deeper. Really try to feel walking 148 miles a year carrying thirty-five tons. Water had to be pumped from a well or collected from a surface water source into a bucket or pail and then carried into the home for any cooking, cleaning, or

15   *Lexico powered by Oxford,* s.v. "quality of life(n.)," Accessed April 19, 2020.
16   *TED,* "Robert J. Gordon: The Death of Innovation, The End of Growth," April 23, 2013, Video.

bathing. If hot water was needed, it had to be heated on the fireplace, the only heating source for the home. Laundering clothes took two days!

> *On Sunday evenings, a housewife soaked clothing in tubs of warm water. When she woke up the next morning, she had to scrub the laundry on a rough washboard and rub it with soap made from lye, which severely irritated her hands. Next, she placed the laundry in big vats of boiling water and stirred the clothes about with a long pole to prevent the clothes from developing yellow spots. Then she lifted the clothes out of the vats with a washstick, rinsed the clothes twice, once in plain water and once with bluing, wrung the clothes out and hung them out to dry. At this point, clothes would be pressed with heavy flatirons and collars would be stiffened with starch.*[17]

Two days and arduous manual labor to do the laundry. Remember, the household was a dirty, relatively dark place.

> *The soot and smoke from coal and wood burning stoves blackened walls and dirtied drapes and carpets. Gas and kerosene lamps left smelly deposits of black soot on furniture and curtains. Each day, the lamp's glass chimneys had to be wiped and wicks trimmed or replaced.*[18]

---

17   Steven Mintz and Sara McNeil, Housework in Late 19th Century America, *Digital History,* Accessed February 23, 2020.

18   Ibid.

For a perspective of life in 1862 America, here is an account from Gro Svendsen, a Norwegian immigrant, astonished by how hard the typical American housewife had to work:

> We are told that the women of America have much leisure time, but I haven't yet met any woman who thought so! Here the mistress of the house must do all the work that the cook, the maid, and the housekeeper would do in an upper-class family at home. Moreover, she must do her work as well as these three together do it in Norway.[19]

And this description was life for white Americans. This book cannot do justice to the exploration of the suffering and challenges of non-white Americans, either then or now. That is another conversation. Just 100 years ago, my grandpa, Hugh Wilson, was born at a time when mules were used to plow the fields, and horses were the main form of transportation. Gordon goes on to describe how prior to the motor vehicle, one-quarter of US agricultural land was used to feed horses that were then in turn used for transportation.

By 1930, my grandpa and his family had to leave their land in Arkansas and move to Dallas to survive the Great Depression. Life was not easy in Dallas, but thanks to the changes brought during this special decade, there was a place to go and escape the despair of their farm. As life improved for him in Dallas, my grandpa eventually ended up attending a county fair and saw his first airplane.

---

19   Ibid.

Invented and built by the Wright brothers and flown by them first in 1903, the airplane, like so many of his contemporaries, had my grandpa completely overcome by the spell and allure of powered flight. He had a lifelong love affair with all things aeronautical. It also led to his heartbreak when, during his physical to enter the US Army Air Corps, the doctor doing his medical examination discovered a perforated eardrum, immediately disqualifying his service. I'm told he was never the same again. He eventually ended up getting his private license, but it wasn't in service of his country.

Over the course of the twentieth century, my grandpa did see invention after invention radically alter everyday life, and in 1969, watched as Neil Armstrong and Buzz Aldrin stepped foot on the surface of the moon. As Armstrong so famously said, "That's one **small** step for man, one giant leap for mankind" (**there must be something to these simple acts**). When I was hired at NASA in 1994, it created a special bond for me with my grandpa. I reveled in the opportunities to share things I learned at work with him, and he remained fascinated by and curious about all things flight up until his death in 2009.

Exploring change on decadal time frames is particularly useful during this special century because the rate of change was so rapid. Hibbard et al. consider the "Great Acceleration" to be the period after World War II and describe how after 1950:

> *"Dramatic changes and even switches in the rates and feedbacks of human enterprise and its associated environmental signatures have occurred...and can broadly be defined as changes in (a) human knowledge, science,*

and technologies, (b) energy systems development, (c) human populations and their demography, (d) production and consumption, and (e) political and economic structures and institutions."[20]

As we are improving our quality of life, we are also impacting the physical world in ways and at a scale not previously possible in such short geological time frames. We have managed to push the size of the systems we operate in from households and proximate local communities to the entire globe and low-earth orbit and have connected nearly every second of every day to all of that in less than 200 hundred years. Let that one sink into your body.

Where do you feel that in your body?

"What makes the period of 1870-1970 so special is that these inventions cannot be repeated."[21] Gordon is building the case for the scope of the threat we face. Since the century was so special and the growth rates were only made possible by inventions creating changes in quality of life that can't be repeated, we are starting to acutely experience problems and challenges that operate within systems at scales beyond our ability to physically connect with in any managed way. It is starting to seriously damage our quality of life ("the

---

20 Kathy A. Hibbard et al. "Group Report: Decadal-scale Interactions of Humans and the Environment," in *Sustainability or Collapse?*, ed. Robert Constanza et al (Cambridge: The MIT Press, 2007), 342.

21 Robert J. Gordon, *The Rise and Fall of American Growth*, (Princeton: Princeton University Press, 2016) Page 4.

standard of health, comfort, and happiness experienced by an individual or group"). While I grew up with the threat of nuclear war, today,

> *transitions to new energy systems are required. There is a growing disparity between wealthy and poor, and through modern communication, a growing awareness by the poor of this gap, which has created a potentially explosive situation. Many of the ecosystem services upon which human well-being depends are degrading, with possible rapid changes when thresholds are crossed. The climate may be more sensitive to increases in carbon dioxide and may have more in-built momentum than earlier thought, raising concerns of abrupt and irreversible changes in the planetary environment as a whole.*[22]

It shouldn't be surprising in the context of human development that things feel so unsettled; the world is so complex. Things **are really unsettled and complex**, and we have had no time on an evolutionary scale to be prepared for it. Less than two hundred years ago, our lives were defined by our physical homes. Now we can know nearly limitless bounds.

Think a little bit more about the changes from the special century and explore how it makes you feel and where you feel it.

---

22 Robert Constanza et al. "Sustainability or Collapse Lessons from Integrating the History of Humans and the Rest of Nature," in *Sustainability or Collapse?*, ed. Robert Constanza et al (Cambridge: The MIT Press, 2007), 10.

When electricity made it possible to create light with the flick of a switch instead of the strike of a match, the process of creating light was changed forever. When the electric elevator allowed buildings to extend vertically instead of horizontally, the very nature of land use was changed, and urban density was created.... Transportation...is noteworthy for achieving 100 percent of its potential increase in speed in little more than a century, from the first primitive railroads replacing the stagecoach in the 1830s to the Boeing 707 flying near the speed of sounds in 1958....Some measures of progress are subjective, but lengthened life expectancy and the conquest of infant mortality are solid quantitative indicators of the advances made over the special century in the realms of medicine and public health.[23]

No wonder there is a strong nostalgia for the post-World War II era. Quality of life was on the rise for most, and with it, a world of possibility. That is no longer the case. "Americans can no longer expect to double the living standard of their parents."[24]

Progress after 1970 continued, but focused more narrowly on entertainment, communication, and information technology in which areas of progress did not arrive with a great and sudden burst as had the by-products of the Great Inventions. Instead, changes

---

23   Robert J. Gordon, *The Rise and Fall of American Growth,* (Princeton: Princeton University Press, 2016) Page 4.

24   *TED,* "Robert J. Gordon: The Death of Innovation, The End of Growth," April 23, 2013, Video, 12:11.

have been evolutionary and continuous....Outside the
sphere of entertainment, communications, and infor-
mation technology, progress was much slower after
1970. Motor vehicles in 2015 accomplish the same basic
role of transporting people and cargo as they did in
1970, albeit with greater convenience and safety. Air
travel today is even less comfortable than it was in
1970. Progress in medicine has also slowed after 1970
compared to the enormous advances made between
1940 and 1970.[25]

Ouch. This stagnation is probably why innovation has become such a buzzword these days. We are looking to squeeze out a little bit more productivity or get people to adopt more slightly efficient practices these days. When searching Amazon for books on "innovation," over 50,000 results came up. I'm going to use my teacher Bob Dunham's definition of innovation: *Innovation is the adoption of new practice in a community.*[26] I love it. It is simple and elegant.

However, since the special century, the improvements in quality of life have been minor. Sadly, rather than spreading quality of life, resources are being concentrated at the very top, while most are left trying to "keep up with the Joneses" and further cycling into states of discomfort and disease. As we chase material happiness, we are sacrificing health and comfort.

---

25 Robert J. Gordon, *The Rise and Fall of American Growth*, (Princeton: Princeton University Press, 2016) Page 7.

26 Peter J. Denning and Robert Dunham, *The Innovator's Way*, (Cambridge: The MIT Press, 2010), 30.

Please don't get me wrong. I'm grateful for the health and comfort I have been afforded. I have a beautiful home that protects me from the elements and is stocked with food and drink to last weeks. I enjoy clean air in a very peaceful, quiet neighborhood and have hot and cold clean running water, trash pickup, and sewer service. These resources are also with loving relationships that nurture and support me. Compared with my great-great-grandparents, only four generations ago, I'm in the aristocracy. And that is here in the United States.

When we zoom out and consider the developing world, many people and places haven't started their own special century of transformation.

According to a World Health Organization/UNICEF 2019 Report:[27]

- 2.2 billion people lack access to safely managed drinking water services.
- Over half of the global population or 4.2 billion people lack safely managed sanitation services.
- 297,000 children under five die every year from diarrhoeal diseases due to poor sanitation, poor hygiene, or unsafe drinking water.

and the International Energy Agency 2019 Report:[28]

---

27   "Water, Sanitation and Hygiene," United Nations, Accessed February 23, 2020.

28   International Energy Agency, "SDG7: Data and Projections," *Flagship Report,* November 2019, Accessed February 23. 2020.

- In 2018, 860 million people still lack access to energy, even though since 2010, 800 million have gotten connected.
- Over 2.6 billion people do not have access to clean cooking facilities.

and from the UN effort to end poverty:[29]

- 736 million people lived below the international poverty line of US $1.90 a day in 2015.
- In 2018, almost 8 percent of the world's workers and their families lived on less than $1.90 per person per day.
- As of 2018, 55 percent of the world's population has no access to at least one social protection cash benefit.

How do those stats make you feel? I'm guessing for many, they don't actually create any meaningful feeling. Numbers like that, at a scale like that, are just too hard to relate to and potentially don't cause a profound or noticeable feeling, or maybe just cause numbness. The numbers sound terrible, but for me, I get more overwhelmed by the number than by the fact that each one those numbers is actually a person!

When I get overwhelmed, I'm not inspired to take action because I can't relate to billions of people or even millions of people. I can relate to one or two, or even a family. I can only relate to as many other people as I commonly interact with, so that's my measure for breaking these large-scale, systemic realities we now face and are connected with into simpler, more familiar relationships.

---

29 "Ending Poverty," United Nations, Accessed February 23, 2020.

Of all the systems I'm personally connected with or the global threats and challenges I might be passionate or concerned about, how do I connect to those systems? Where is my relationship with them, how does it work, and what do I have responsibility for? When I can understand the answers to those questions, align them with my own "for the sake of what" and connect both the understanding and purpose of others, we are talking about real systemic change, and that is a powerful force.

Since I get overwhelmed by such big numbers, I'd like to explore a big number potentially easier to manage. This number comes from a factoid that stands out in my memory from my time working at NASA. It is not a number much easier to comprehend, but it is an order of magnitude smaller and it's easier on the heart and soul, as it is about human spaceflight. From the time the solid rocket motors for the Space Shuttle splashed down in the Atlantic Ocean, there were more than one million steps to get the Space Shuttle ready to fly again.

Now I never asked if there were a million and one steps or two million steps. My mind stopped at one million because I just couldn't relate to a number that big. One thing I do with big numbers is break them down into smaller numbers and ideally to things I can relate to. Let's try some:

- It takes more than eleven and half days, nearly two weeks, to reach one million seconds.
- According to the Cleveland Clinic, the normal number of breaths taken per minute for resting adults is between twelve and twenty. If one were to remain at rest, it would

take 57.8 days, nearly two months, of twelve breaths per minute to reach one million breaths.[30]

- According to the Mayo Clinic, the average American walks three thousand to four thousand steps a day.[31] At three thousand steps per day, it will take 333.33 days, nearly a year, to reach one million steps.

Breaking down a million like that is a bit better, but doesn't really help much. It is still a bunch of numbers. Those million actions to get the Space Shuttle ready to fly again were taken and acted on by someone. There was a well-choreographed effort of individuals coming together for something bigger than that one millionth step. Each of the individuals in that process had relationships with others in the system, and they aligned their efforts to get the Space Shuttle ready to launch again. There was a multitude of relationships organized around the goal of safely launching the Space Shuttle again.

Before we continue into outer space, let's bring it back home to our bodies, our biology, and our lizard brain.

CHAPTER SUMMARY

In the history of humankind, we live in a time when we can enjoy the benefits of the greatest period of improvement in quality of life, and yet we are still suffering and struggling to provide basic services to hundreds of millions of people. Rather than enjoying and sharing in the bounty, we are sacrificing our well-being, operating systems that don't

---

30   "Vital Signs," Cleveland Clinic, Accessed February 23, 2020.

31   Thom Rieck, "10,000 steps a day: Too low? Too high?", *Mayo Clinic*, Accessed February 23, 2020.

fully serve our needs, and struggling with the complexity and overwhelm these systemic breakdowns create. As a first step, let's begin by exploring how these breakdowns feel in our bodies and where we feel them. This exploration is preparing us for our next conversation about biology in Chapter Three.

CHAPTER THREE

THE LIZARD BRAIN?

———

In 1954, the limbic cortex was described by neuroanatomists. Since that time, the limbic system of the brain has been implicated as the seat of emotion, addiction, mood, and lots of other mental and emotional processes. It is the part of the brain that is phylogenetically very primitive. Many people call it the "Lizard Brain," because the limbic system is about all a lizard has for brain function. It is in charge of fight, flight, feeding, fear, freezing up, and fornication.[32]

The theory of the lizard, mammalian, and Homo sapien brains or "Triune Brain" has been proven inaccurate, yet the term "Lizard Brain" stuck with me years ago. For our purposes, we will focus on the limbic system rather a particular brain type. Indulge my connection to the "Lizard Brain" for a slight detour.

When I hear Lizard Brain, I think of Jim Morrison, lead singer of The Doors. Every time I think about The Doors,

---

32 Joseph Troncale, "Your Lizard Brain," *Psychology Today*, April 22, 2014, Accessed May 31, 2020.

I hear their song, "Riders on the Storm." I can even feel a tingle on my skin. The rain slowly falling and the thunder in the background at the beginning transports me out to the American West. Sometimes I can even smell the desert of Tucson as the desert responds to the overdue and welcome drink. Glorious.

Sadly, "Riders on the Storm" was the last song ever recorded by The Doors and Jim Morrison's whispering in the background was the last recording of him in the studio. You may not have known the whispering is there. It's worth going back to listen to. Here is recording engineer Bruce Botnick describing the recording experience:

> It's hard to remember the exact chronology—unfortunately a lot of the tape boxes and outtakes were destroyed—but 'Riders On The Storm', like everything else, took only two or three takes and, as an afterthought, we recorded Jim's whispered vocal. We all thought of the idea for the sound effects and Jim was the one who first said it out loud: 'Wouldn't it be cool to add rain and thunder?' I used the Elektra sound effects recordings and, as we were mixing, I just pressed the button. Serendipity worked so that all the thunder came in at all the right places. It took you somewhere. It was like a mini movie in our heads.[33]

I make connections from hearing Lizard Brain to my personal movie flashback of lightning striking in the mountains

---

33 Mick Houghton, "The Making Of... The Doors' Riders On The Storm," *Uncut,* February 2007 issue, Take 117, Accessed February 25, 2020.

in the distance, backlighting a saguaro cactus with two arms uplifted and forming a triad with the centerpiece. For me, imagining a magical rainstorm in Tucson back in 2002, there is clearly a lot happening in that brain of ours.

In her 2009 *National Geographic* article, Catherine Zuckerman states, "Weighing in at three pounds, on average, the human brain is more complex than any other known structure in the universe."[34] The National Institutes of Health (NIH) curriculum supplement informs that "the brain makes up only 2 percent of our body weight, but it consumes 20 percent of the oxygen we breathe and 20 percent of the energy we consume. This enormous consumption of oxygen and energy fuels many thousands of chemical reactions in the brain every second. These chemical reactions underlie the actions and behaviors we use to respond to our environment."[35]

How are we responding to our environment? Sadly, many are not responding well.

According to the National Institute of Mental Health (NIMH), in 2017

- There were an estimated 46.6 million adults aged eighteen or older in the United States with a mental, behavioral, or emotional disorder. This number represented 18.9 percent of all US adults.

---

34 Catherine Zuckerman, "The human brain, explained," National Geographic, October 15, 2009, Accessed February 25, 2020. "

35 "Information About the Brain," National Institute of Health Curriculum Supplement Series [Internet], Accessed February 25, 2020.

- The prevalence of mental, behavioral, or emotional disorders was higher among women (22.3 percent) than men (15.1 percent).
- Young adults aged eighteen to twenty-five years had the highest prevalence of mental, behavioral, or emotional disorder (25.8 percent) compared to adults aged twenty-six to forty-nine years (22.2 percent) and aged fifty and older (13.8 percent).[36]

According to the Centers for Disease Control and Prevention (CDC):

> *Mental health disorders are among the most burdensome health concerns in the United States with 71 percent of adults reporting at least one symptom of stress, such as a headache or feeling overwhelmed or anxious. Many people with mental health disorders also need care for other physical health conditions, including heart disease, diabetes, respiratory illness, and disorders that affect muscles, bones, and joints. The costs for treating people with both mental health disorders and other physical conditions are two to three times higher than for those without co-occurring illnesses. By combining medical and behavioral healthcare services, the United States could save $37.6 billion to $67.8 billion a year.*[37]

---

36 "Mental Illness," National Institute of Mental Health, Accessed February 25, 2020.

37 "Mental Health in the Workplace," Centers for Disease Control and Prevention, Accessed February 25, 2020.

The NIMH found just over 7 percent of US adults had a major depressive episode in 2017.[38] A 2016 Blue Cross Blue Shield report found a 33 percent increase in the diagnosis of major depression compared with 2013, and shockingly youth aged twelve to seventeen experienced a 63 percent increase over that same time period.[39]

"Two in five Americans report that they sometimes or always feel their social relationships are not meaningful, and one in five say they feel lonely or socially isolated." According to the US Census Bureau, over one-quarter of the population and 28 percent of older adults now live by themselves.[40]

This is some tough data to process. Not only are the numbers big, but they indicate a lot of suffering and loneliness. We can change!

Research into the brain's ability to adapt and change is providing some remarkable new understanding. "Scientific investigations have demonstrated that even the adult brain generates new neurons within a region important for learning and memory. The brain's ability to change and reorganize in response to some input is known as plasticity. Plasticity is defined by a change in the anatomy of the neuron. New synapses may form, existing synapses may strengthen, some synapses may be eliminated...."[41]

---

38 "Major Depression," National Institute of Mental Health, Accessed February 25, 2020.

39 Maggie Fox, "Major depression on the rise among everyone, new data shows," NBC News, May 11, 2018, Accessed February 25, 2020.

40 "The Loneliness Epidemic," Health Resources and Services Administration, Accessed February 25, 2020.

41 "Information About the Brain," National Institute of Health Curriculum Supplement Series [Internet], Accessed February 25, 2020.

Given the complexity of the world, where cause and effect are not predictable, the ability to rewire our brains seems to have become even more important. We can no longer solely rely on our past experiences to guide our present actions. To navigate this new world order, we need the ability to act from **presence**.

I had the great privilege to study with and get to know the gifted Doug Silsbee before his much too early passing. In his last book, *Presence-Based Leadership: Complexity Practices for Clarity, Resilience, and Results That Matter*, he defines presence as "an internal state: the awareness of immediacy, stillness, inclusive awareness, and possibility. This state enables us to sense the world as it actually is and to sense ourselves as we actually are. A rigorous embrace of reality leads to clarity, resilience, and results that matter."[42]

Doug lists these new realities contributing to our complex world:

> *Historical stability seems to vanish. Globalization, intensified competition, the need to do more with less, disruptive technologies, climate change, resource scarcities, economic disenfranchisement, macroeconomic sea changes, and political paralysis can give rise to a real sense that the world is hurtling towards chaos.*[43]

---

42 Doug Silsbee, "*Presence-Based Leadership: Complexity Practices for Clarity, Resilience, and Results That Matter,*" (Asheville: Yes! Global Inc., 2018), Preface.

43 Ibid, Introduction.

It sure can feel that way to me.

I'd like to go a little deeper and explore how psychoanalysis was used to create modern public relations. Larry Tye's *The Father of Spin* explores the life of Edward L. Bernays, often recognized as the Father of Public Relations, and how Bernays changed the world. Bernays was the nephew of the revolutionary and world-famous psychologist Sigmund Freud, and as we are exploring the practices to access the present moment, it felt important to inform you about Bernays. In the preface of Tye's book, he states:

> *If housewives could be guided in their selection of soap, so could husbands in their choice of a car. And voters in their selection of candidates. And candidates in their political posturing. Indeed, the very substance of American thought was merely clay to be molded by the savvy public relations practitioner, or so it seemed.*

> *With the stakes so high, however, even Bernays needed help. He turned to his uncle, Sigmund Freud. Much as Freud had revolutionized the way the world thought about individual behavior, Bernays was able to transform attitudes toward group action. He used his uncle's ideas in the commercial realm to predict, then adjust, the way people believed and then behaved. Never mind that they didn't realize it. In fact, all the better. And just as Freud was rewarded with the title Father of Psychoanalysis, so Bernays became known around the world as the Father of Public Relations.[44]*

44 Larry Tye, "*The Father of Spin,*" (New York: Crown Publishers, 1998), Preface.

As technology has progressed, we find ourselves at even greater risk. Michael Kosinski's research, meant as a warning, explains why. His work is described on the Stanford University website below.

> As a doctoral student and deputy director at Cambridge University Psychometrics Center from 2008 to 2014, Kosinski worked with a colleague to investigate whether it was possible to identify people's psychological traits from their Facebook "likes."
>
> People who "liked" Battlestar Galactica were likely to be introverts, for example, while people who "liked" Lady Gaga were likely to be extroverts. Kosinski and his Cambridge colleague, David Stillwell, were able to correlate "likes" with other basic personality traits: openness, conscientiousness, agreeableness, and neuroticism. Armed with only ten "likes," they could evaluate a person's traits more accurately than that person's coworkers. With seventy "likes," they could do better than a person's close friends.
>
> And now, in a new study, Kosinski and his colleagues — including Stillwell, Sandra Matz of Columbia Business School, and Gideon Nave of Wharton School of Business — confirm the next logical step: ads are indeed more persuasive when they are tailored to those psychological traits.[45]

---

45 Edmund Andrews, "The Science Behind Cambridge Analytica: Does Psychological Profiling Work?", Stanford Graduate School of Business, April 12, 2018, Accessed February 27, 2020.

In an interview, Kosinski goes on to say "using digital technologies you leave behind an enormous amount of digital footprints. In fact, it has been recently estimated that an average human leaves a few gigabytes of data footprint every single day. And what I think people also haven't realized yet fully is that those digital footprints can be analyzed by algorithms to extract a lot of secondary data."[46]

Clearly, people are suffering, and this world we've created for ourselves is complex in many dimensions. The money we earn doesn't go as far, yet we are compelled to consume more. In this hyperconnected world, we are likely spending more time working in our jobs than actually connecting with our friends and loved ones in meaningful ways. We can also feel many things happening in the global context that we are not actually connected to, but merely pawns being played in a bigger game.

And yes, there is shit happening in the world bigger than us. This has always been the case. Even when our connected world was just a single home or when we cherished fire in a cave, life was simple. We can just see it more clearly now as we leave our digital footprints on our journey.

I suspect this connectivity is why conspiracy theories are so effective. We feel something from this disconnected vulnerability, and it feels sinister. We want to have control or at least some explanation. Surely, if someone I "trust" says and shares this conspiracy theory, I can trust it.

---

46 *ACADEMIA SUPERIOR - Gesellschaft für Zukunftsforschung - Institute for Future Studies,* "You are the product!" April 15, 2019. Video, 6:19.

The personal mishap I had with these reactive, unconnected, and ungrounded thoughtless conspiracy thoughts proves to be a regular reminder of my own human fallacy. On Wednesday, July 17, 1996, it is a balmy summer night with temperatures in the mid-80s at John F. Kennedy Airport in Queens, New York.

> *Shortly after takeoff from New York's Kennedy International Airport, a TWA Boeing 747 jetliner bound for Paris explodes over the Atlantic Ocean, killing all 230 people aboard. Flight 800 had just received clearance to initiate a climb to cruise altitude when it exploded without warning. Because the plane was loaded with fuel for the long transatlantic journey, it vaporized within moments, creating a fireball seen almost all along the coastline of Long Island.[47]*

Thankfully, the total number of airline fatalities are relatively small. According to the US Department of Transportation, in 2018, there were 394 deaths by air travel and 36,560 by highway travel.[48] Nonetheless, when airline fatalities do happen, they are shocking and emotional.

After TWA 800 went down, the country was in shock. People representing ten countries—children, fathers, mothers, siblings—were gone in an instant, and the surviving families and friends were left to process the profound loss. Sadly, that loss was compounded by a conspiracy about the plane getting shot down. None less than Pierre Salinger, President

---

47 "Flight 800 explodes over Long Island," History.com Editors, Accessed February 27, 2020.

48 "Transportation Fatalities by Mode," Bureau of Transportation Statistics, United States Department of Transportation, Accessed February 27, 2020.

John F. Kennedy's press secretary and former network news correspondent, took to the airwaves claiming there was a cover-up underway of an accidental missile launch and the US Navy was responsible.[49] For some reason, Salinger was relying on a discredited document.

Yet when a forwarded email arrived at my official NASA email address supporting Salinger's claim, I mindlessly took the time to forward that email from my official NASA account to a large list of friends and family. In less than three hours, I received a message from a Navy official asking if the email I had sent was NASA's official position. Horrified, receiving that Navy email physically felt like getting hit in the gut.

After recovering from the punch and the deeper realization of what I had done, I quickly responded that definitely not, this was in no way an official NASA position. I then proceeded to email all those to whom I had forwarded Salinger's claim to explain my thoughtless action. I felt terrible not just for myself, but for all those impacted by the loss of their loved ones and how my carelessness might contribute to their suffering.

NASA's official position? How terrible. That experience focused for me how powerful and problematic our thoughtless actions could be. After that experience, I strive to take the time to consider what I forward and try to imagine if my recipients would be affected positively or negatively.

Our brains are effective because they support us to be decision-making machines, which can literally save our lives. Our

---

49   Jeffrey Reid, "Pierre Salinger Syndrome and the TWA 800 Conspiracies," *CNN*, July 17, 2006, Accessed February 27, 2020.

decision-making is also a superpower every one of us has. No need to turn to the great Stan Lee. We are all superheroes.

This shared power is the very mundane power of choice. What I find even cooler is that as superheroes, we can actually train our powers. There has been a lot of excellent research done on the topic of habits, and I'm happy to point in the direction of James Clear's work *Atomic Habits*.

What an excellent read and practice for those interested in stopping "bad" habits or starting new "good" habits. Clear shares his beautiful perspective and experience with habits and provides tools to become aware of our current habits and how to support creating new ones. Full of steps we can take to support the habits we choose, it is very practical. These practices can be useful as we embark on new practices of simple acts.

Let's end with a perfect quote from Lao Tzu that Clear shares in *Atomic Habits* before turning to the practices of simple acts.

Humans are born soft and supple;
dead, they are stiff and hard.
Plants are born tender and pliant;
dead, they are brittle and dry.
Thus, whoever is stiff and inflexible
is a disciple of death.
Whoever is soft and yielding
is a disciple of life.
The hard and stiff will be broken.
The soft and supple will prevail.[50]

50   James Clear, *"Atomic Habits,"* (New York: Avery, 2018), 193.

CHAPTER SUMMARY

As complex and puzzling as the brain may be, it can be **rewired**, which is fortunate because the world around us can feel increasingly more complex. Within this **complex world**, there are people trying to manipulate us. Within our digital world, we are leaving clues for others to use these **digital footprints** to extract all sorts of insights about us. Take care and think about what you are forwarding and the **impact** it might have **on others**. Take a moment and thank your "lizard brain" before we move on to the simple acts and training our superpowers.

SECTION TWO

CHAPTER FOUR

THE POWER OF NOW

———

In 1997, at age twenty-nine, Eckhart Tolle, the now famous spiritual teacher, had just matriculated at Cambridge University as a postgraduate student, which is quite remarkable because he refused any formal education from ages fifteen to twenty-two. And this is *the* Cambridge University, the second oldest English-speaking university in the world, founded in 1209. Some of the world's greatest scientists and significant breakthroughs are associated with Cambridge: Jane Goodall, Sir Isaac Newton, Charles Darwin, Francis Crick, and Stephen Hawking, to name just a few.[51] Having reached one of the institutional pinnacles of intellectual achievement, Tolle was struggling. He was unhappy, anxious, and depressed. He was searching for answers, but he was looking to his intellect to find a way through his pain.

Then, in a moment of clarity, he saw through his pain and felt relief and was deeply at peace.

---

51 Innovation Cities, "Eight Cambridge alumni who shook the world," *CNBC,* September 30, 2014, Accessed April 25, 2020.

Suddenly I stepped back from myself, and it seemed to be two of me. The 'I', and this 'self' that I cannot live with. Am I one or am I two? And that triggered me like a koan [a Zen statement that appeals to intuition rather than ration]. It happened to me spontaneously. I looked at that sentence: 'I can't live with myself'. I had no intellectual answer. Who am I? Who is this self that I cannot live with? The answer came on a deeper level. I realized who I was.[52]

He spent the next two years sitting on park benches and writing his first book, *The Power of Now: A Guide to Spiritual Enlightenment.* In it, Tolle is inviting us to reimagine Descartes's proclamation, "I think, therefore I am"[53] to separate our thinking self from our essence.

As William Bloom, a former professor at the London School of Economics and one of the United Kingdom's most experienced teachers, healers, and authors in the field of holistic development, told the Independent in 2008 when asked about Tolle, "he asks people to exist as best they can in any given moment and to connect with the sensation of the physical body–so instead of just staying in your head thinking, to be aware of what's happening in your feet, your hands, your whole body."[54] This shift is really challenging because Descartes's philosophy has so rooted itself in our culture,

52 Ether Walker, "Eckhart Tolle: This man could change your life," *Independent,* June 21, 2008, Accessed April 25, 2020.

53 *Encyclopaedia Britannica Online,* s.v. "René Descartes," accessed April 25, 2020.

54 Ether Walker, "Eckhart Tolle: This man could change your life," *Independent,* June 21, 2008, Accessed April 25, 2020.

and as described earlier in the book, the complexity of our world so often takes us out of our body.

The simple practices we are going to explore have helped me to become more present in the moment: more grounded in my body and more confident and comfortable in navigating through the vagaries of my life. These simple practices have helped me to connect more meaningfully and deeply with others. They have provided me with a great satisfaction and source for joyful happiness. What I also find so exciting about these practices is they don't take a lot of work. They help me plug into the moment and then feel the empowerment of possibility and choice.

It is not surprising to me that Oprah Winfrey connected with Tolle and developed an in-depth web series with him because she has been guided by her feeling self. One of her greatest gifts has been her sharing of Eckhart Tolle and his beautiful teachings with a mainstream audience.

Back in 1958, when Oprah was four, she knew her life would be different. She was watching her grandmother boil the clothes to do the laundry, and she just felt it in her body that her life would be different.[55] By age nineteen, she was working in TV in Nashville, Tennessee. She was the ten p.m. anchor reading the news. She was still in college and making $10,000 a year, but it didn't totally feel "right." Then she got an offer to move to Atlanta for $40,000. Her boss in Nashville counseled her that she was

---

55 *Evan Carmichael*, "Oprah Winfrey's INSPIRING Story," November 18, 2017, video, 21:20.

not ready. He told her she needed to learn to write better and perfect her craft. He couldn't match the $40,000 but did offer her a $2,000 raise. Again, Oprah felt into her body and realized her boss was absolutely right. She did need to keep learning.

This realization helped her on her journey to start "listening" to what felt right. A couple of years later, at twenty-two, Oprah moved to Baltimore and was making $22,000 a year as an anchor. While her father and her friends told her she shouldn't give up being an anchor, it didn't feel right. By the time she was making $25,000 a year, her father told her, "You've hit the jackpot and aren't going to make any more money than that."[56]

Yes, this is Oprah Winfrey, who, according to Forbes, as of April 25, 2020, was worth $2.6 billion.[57] She felt this conflict about her career. The external world (family and friends) was telling her one thing and she was feeling something very different in her body. She said being a reporter, "felt like an unnatural act" even though to the world it was "glamorous."[58] She was struggling with uncertainty. Winfrey said, "Knowing what you don't want to do is the best possible place to be if you don't know what to do, because knowing what you don't want to do leads you to figure out what you really do want to do."[59]

---

56 *Stanford Graduate School of Business*, "Oprah Winfrey on Career, Life, and Leadership," April 28, 2014, video 1:04:03.

57 *Forbes*, "Real Time Net Worth," accessed April 25, 2020.

58 *Stanford Graduate School of Business*, "Oprah Winfrey on Career, Life, and Leadership," April 28, 2014, video 1:04:03.

59 Ibid.

For some reason, Winfrey got "demoted" to a talk show! Since she was under contract, the station still wanted to try to get some work out of her through the end of the year. The moment she sat down to conduct her first interview with the Carvel Ice Cream (remember Fudgie the Whale by any chance?) man who talked about his multiple flavors, Oprah knew she had "found home for herself." Her bottom-line message is that all her best decisions in life have come from listening to her instinct. Oprah said she was attuned "to what really felt like the next right move for me."[60]

Oprah got a call to move to Chicago, where Phil Donahue, the reigning king of talk shows, was located. Every single person in her world except her one friend told her not to go because she would fail. Even her bosses, who had come to love and respect her, told her Chicago was a racist city and, as a black woman, she was going to fail. They felt so strongly that they began offering her incentives to stay. But Oprah stayed true to what felt right to her and thought if she did actually fail, then that process would help her figure out what was the next thing for her.

While her contemporaries in news were very prepared with their tapes and stories and resumes ready, Winfrey didn't prepare that way. She knew what was relevant would show up when she needed it. Her definition of luck is "preparation meeting the moment of opportunity."[61] Oprah knew she was prepared to step into the world of talk.

---

60 Ibid.
61 Ibid.

The experience of feeling can be elusive. We are not taught much about "feelings." Often we are told to pack them away. Feelings are messy and don't fit into nice, well-defined boxes because they are subjective. Feelings are our own sensations. It can be hard to find an objective "truth" about our feelings that aligns with the feelings of others. Feelings are really just assessments of what is going on in our body, yet because they are happening in our body, they feel like assertions.

Assertions are objective facts, like, "It is seventy-two degrees in this room." We can walk over to a thermostat and see it is registering seventy-two degrees on the thermometer and agree to the assertion about the temperature. But when I say it is hot in here, that is my own feeling and assessment of what it feels like in the room. To my wife, seventy-two may feel cold, but to me, it can feel hot. For me an upset stomach means a burning sensation, while for others it may mean bowel problems or even a nervous feeling of butterflies.

Since we don't typically have a lot of experience with really feeling something and having the confidence and language to describe our assessment of the feeling, communicating feelings can lead to lots of disconnect and frustration. We don't have or use precise language to describe the feeling, or we assume it is the same experience for others. These disconnects can then make it more likely we will shift back to thinking about the experience and away from the feeling of the experience. Getting some practice with feelings is an important part of this journey and will help underpin the other practices throughout the book.

Take a moment to feel wherever your body is contacting. Is it the ground or some support? Maybe it is your feet on the floor or ground, your butt on a seat, or your back against the chair. Maybe you are drawn to your hands and fingers holding this book or e-reader. If you are holding this book, then it is likely hard to move your attention beyond your fingertips, as research has shown they are the most sensitive parts of the body for discerning pain and touch.[62]

My invitation is to notice whatever part of your body you feel supporting you. Notice the sensation felt at the boundary between your body and the external world. As you begin to notice that feeling, you might feel a tingle. You might feel heat or cold. You might feel numbness. You might feel a subtle movement. You might not feel anything. The importance is not to feel anything expected or what I've described, but to take the time to begin drawing your attention to that boundary and put your own definition to that sensation. This sensation is one of the many interfaces you have with the physical world, and these connections are happening all the time.

What I find so powerful and amazing is if you can feel something or even notice the slightest sensation, you are in the present moment. This is what presence feels like! We can train our awareness to become more comfortable with these sensations, more comfortable with our own bodies. Feelings are not as we think they should be, but as they are—as Tolle would say, the "isness."

---

62 'Flavia Mancini et al., "Whole-Body Mapping of Spatial Acuity for Pain and Touch," *Annals of neurology,* 75(6), (Jun 2014): 917.

This practice is the simplest way to access the present moment that I know of. We can practice it all the time throughout our day. Walking, by feeling our feet connect to the ground. Sitting, by feeling our bodies on the chair. Preparing dinner, by feeling the chef's knife in our hand. Loving, by feeling the body of a loved one when we hug and hold one another. Can you access some part of your body right now, contacting the support of the chair or ground?

I have found this practice really helpful in getting me out of my head. I used to be VERY self-conscious about public speaking. Even speaking up in meetings was hard for me. I would jump on my thought train and start thinking about how I might embarrass myself or ask a dumb question. Believe me, I have had good experience asking dumb questions.

So I began a practice of wiggling my toes to get me into my body and out of my head. As soon as I started wiggling my toes, I moved from my head and the negative thoughts about what "might" happen and into my body to feel what was happening. What I love about this practice is that it is one no one has to see (unless you are in flip-flops or barefoot), so it can be a stealth superpower in finding the present moment. The power of now, being in the present moment, is a truly beneficial simple act.

CHAPTER SUMMARY

Feelings are the subjective experience we are having in our bodies. Because of their subjectivity and our imprecise use of language that in itself is insufficient to describe the experience, feelings are messy. Feelings are further complicated by centuries of reinforced belief about the superiority of thinking. No wonder we have difficulty feeling into our bodies. Yet these feelings can be powerful guides. Just look at Oprah's success. The simple acts central to this book are opportunities to practice with feeling and help us to more easily feel the present moment. Let's move on to the power of feeling our breath.

CHAPTER FIVE

WHERE IS YOUR BREATH?

———

Breath. It is always with us. To breathe is to be alive. It is one of the first things we do at birth and one of the last things we do in our lives. It happens without us thinking about it. And maybe because of this constant companion, we often take it for granted.

Yet we do have the power to choose to control our breathing. We can hold our breath, either on the inhale or the exhale. We can change the rhythm of our inhalation and exhalation. We can breathe more deeply or more shallowly. With CPR, we can even share our breath to keep another alive.

Our breath is critical to life because it brings oxygen (O_2) into the body through the lungs and exchanges it with carbon dioxide (CO_2). The O_2 helps us burn the sugars and the fatty acids in our cells for energy. Because it is so critical, it is generally accepted that some of your brain cells will start to die after depriving your body of O_2 for five minutes or even fewer.[63]

The topic takes me back to a scary moment when I was scuba diving. In 2005, I was given one of the greatest gifts of exploration: a gift certificate for a diving certification. I committed to the classroom time and the pool training and got certified just in time for a trip to the Yucatan in Mexico. I was equally excited because my experience would not be far from where that asteroid struck the earth sixty-six million years ago. Diving provided a way to explore I had only seen on big and little screens. It was now in real-time 3D.

There was the salt taste in my mouth. I was fully aware and connected to my breath. Buoyancy underwater was supported by the gear, and my sensation of sound was significantly reduced, but I have never heard and felt my breath so distinctly. I have certainly had tastier and cleaner breaths in my life, but rarely have I been more fully present in the moment with my breath. As I was exploring this "unnatural" environment underwater, made possible by breathing gear, I was fully aware that breathing gear made it all possible.

Unfortunately, it was a couple of years later until I went on a diving trip again. This next dive was only going to be with a dive master and my brother. The dive master was pretty chill and trusted we were familiar with the techniques and skills. However, it had been years for me. I quickly learned I wasn't ready for a dive without a solid refresher.

---

63   MedlinePlus, "Cerebral Hypoxia," *U.S. National Library of Medicine,* accessed April 25, 2020.

I was the last in the water, and after getting down to about one hundred feet and checking in that all was okay, we headed off on the adventure. Somehow my mask started leaking, so I stopped and lifted the top of the mask to clear it. To my surprise, lifting the top of the mask didn't clear it. It filled it!

I couldn't see anything with my eyes closed, and my panic started to kick in big time. I was down at about one hundred feet, I couldn't see, and I was at the end of the group. It would be some time before they noticed I was not with them. My breathing rate skyrocketed, fear temporarily overwhelmed me, and my limbic system cried out for me to shoot to the surface. We had taken our time coming down to adjust to the depth, so shooting to the surface would have made me very sick and potentially killed me.

It was then my breath training kicked in. I slowed my breath. Enjoying that salty taste, I slowly filled my lungs with air, holding that inhale before slowly exhaling. As calm returned, my diving training kicked in. I lifted the bottom of my mask as I exhaled through my nose and cleared out the water. I opened my eyes and could see again! While it felt like hours, it all happened so quickly. I could see the instructor and my brother ahead of me and easily caught up. In an instant my heart temporarily stopped as I saw my first shark underwater! It was a five-foot reef shark, swimming below me by about twenty feet and fifty feet in the distance. Seeing such graceful, efficient beauty with my heart stopping at the same time is something I will never forget.

To be sure that shocks happened in threes on this dive, as we were returning to the surface and making periodic safety stops for our bodies to adjust to the changing pressure, my brother started doing underwater somersaults to express his enthusiasm and joy for this wonderful dive. Unfortunately, he didn't remember that he would use a bunch more O_2 because of the exertion. After a series of somersaults, he looked down at his O_2 gauge and he was out. His natural reaction was to shoot to the surface. Bad idea. The dive master grabbed him before he could do anything rash and handed him his "octopus" (this is a second mouthpiece that allows another diver to breathe off of your tank). They rose to surface together, safely.

Where is your breath? Where do you feel it?

I invite you to take this moment to notice your own breath. As it happens on its own, can you feel how the body moves to support its flow? Can you feel where the breath touches you? Maybe the entrance of your nose or the back of your throat? Maybe you feel your chest expand or your belly extend? Maybe both? What's magical about noticing where you feel your breath, just like noticing your body and where you feel the sensation of your feet on the ground or the support of your chair, is that it brings you directly into the present moment. Remember what's powerful about being in the present moment is the world is suddenly full of possibilities.

In the early days of working with my breath, I clearly remember asking my teacher, Jill Satterfield, "Should I imagine a cloud of air entering my lungs?"

She was kind and didn't laugh, but it causes me to chuckle to this day as I reflect on how I have a tendency to approach an experience as an intellectual endeavor first. I wanted to let my imagination drive the experience rather than let my *feeling self* experience my breath. It was something outside of me—a concept. I'm grateful for her gentle guidance into my own felt experience and how that helped me internalize my relationship with my breath.

I like to speculate John Glenn was a master of his breath. I never got to ask him about it, but one experience stands out for me about why he might be a master. It was Friday, January 16, 1998, and my boss and mentor, Dan Goldin, was about to announce John Glenn's return to flight. Kathy Sawyer, a reporter for the *Washington Post*, captured it this way:

> *NASA Administrator Daniel S. Goldin yesterday made it official: "I am extremely proud to announce that John Glenn of Ohio, the first American to orbit the earth, will get his long-awaited second flight."*
>
> *Sen. Glenn (D-Ohio), seventy-six, smiled benignly, eyes twinkling, as he claimed his prize at a packed news conference at NASA headquarters with his wife, Annie, watching in the audience. "I see this as another adventure into the unknown," Glenn said. "I guarantee you I'll give it the very best I have."*[64]

---

64   Kathy Sawyer, "NASA Confirms Second Liftoff for First American to Orbit Earth," *Washington Post*, January 17, 1998.

Just before that announcement, I was upstairs at NASA headquarters in the Administrator's suite on the ninth floor as Goldin, Glenn, and others prepared for the news conference. I joined them on the elevator down to the auditorium in the lobby for the press conference to announce Glenn's return to flight. As the group exited the elevator, I held back. Goldin and Glenn turned the corner to walk out into the lobby. Flash bulbs started popping; there was this amazing buzz in the air.

John Glenn was walking out to announce to the world that his long-awaited dream to return to space is happening. And then he stopped. I can only imagine he stopped after he found his breath and turned around to grab his wife Annie's hand and pull her forward into the maelstrom of reporters. As a couple, they were clearly a team. John Glenn included Annie in the announcement. I would like to think his breath helped him find the moment and include her in "his" moment. We'll never know, but breath has the ability to ground us in the moment, even moments as large as that and help us to be our best selves.

Where is your breath? Where do you feel it?

One of my treasured experiences was to teach breath practices and some simple movement exercises with my teacher, Jill Satterfield. I love her perspective: "The body is our house—and how we live in it and where we occupy it are uniquely ours, as well as being part of the common human experience. The body is a treasure trove and an exquisite vehicle for our practice of waking up and being with what is."[65] She integrates mindfulness, somatic awareness, and contemplative psychology in magical ways and currently offers workshops, trainings, retreats, and one-on-one support across the country.

In 2009, Jill invited me to join her down on the Lower East Side of Manhattan at the New York City Health + Hospitals/Gouverneur location to assist in teaching. I was her lead teacher working with a self-selected group of survivors from the 9/11 attacks suffering from post-traumatic stress disorder (PTSD) while she taught a group managing chronic pain. My group met weekly for an hour over the course of many months and the class size varied from two to ten patients.

It was such a beautiful experience, and I was getting direct feedback about the positive difference we were making in the lives of other people. A couple of the participants had to take multiple buses and travel over an hour to get to class and were willing to make the commitment because they were feeling results. It was not a formal medical study, but I was told some of the patients were taking less sleeping medication, attributing the change to the practices we were teaching. That teaching experience lasted less than a year, but confirmed for me the power of simple practices to create tangible, real-world differences.

There are many teachers and traditions working with breath. My purposes in this book are not to dive too deeply into any

---

65   "Our Home of Practice," Jill Satterfield, accessed April 25, 2020.

single practice. Remember this book is about the simple acts we can take. There are many resources in the footnotes and at the back of the book to guide you to amazing teachers like Wim Hof.[66]

I do want to share some research conducted by Patrick McKeown and contained in his book *The Oxygen Advantage: Simple, Scientifically Proven Breathing Techniques to Help You Become Healthier, Slimmer, Faster, and Fitter.*[67] McKeown struggled with asthma since he was a child, and for nearly twenty years, he relied upon medications to manage his symptoms. As a young adult, he had surgery on his nose to help him breathe better, yet he still found himself exhausted and stressed out until he discovered the work of Dr. Konstantin Buteyko. By applying the work of Dr. Buteyko, a Russian physician who had conducted research on optimal breathing for cosmonauts in the Soviet space program, McKeown experienced immediate relief from his asthmatic condition. His experience led to a career change in order to help children and other adults suffering from similar breathing problems.

As McKeown describes, the purpose of breathing is not to just take air into the body, but down into the lungs so the O_2 can be exchanged with CO_2 in the blood. McKeown advocates for breathing through the nose because it naturally takes our breath more deeply into our lungs, where there is more blood exchange potential between O_2 and CO_2 than other parts of the lungs, which helps to oxygenate the blood more effectively

---

66   "Wim Hof Method," Wim Hof, accessed April 25, 2020.
67   Patrick McKeown, *The Oxygen Advantage,* (New York: Harper Collins, 2015).

and efficiently. McKeown uses the Body Oxygen Level Test (BOLT) score to measure the body's response to levels of CO_2 in the blood. Our bodies have evolved to respond to a buildup of CO_2 in the blood, and when it reaches a certain threshold, the body's involuntary response is to take a breath into the lungs. He describes this buildup of CO_2 in the body as an "air hunger."

When McKeown asked groups of his students if they feel more tired than they should be, about 80 percent raised their hands. He "measured the oxygen saturation of thousands of people, and the vast majority display normal blood oxygen saturation of between 95 and 99 percent. Why would this be? Their blood oxygen saturations are normal, yet they constantly feel tired. The problem is not a lack of O_2 in the blood, but that not enough O_2 is being released from the blood to the tissues and organs, including the brain, resulting in feelings of lethargy and exhaustion."[68] He goes on to describe that "[carbon] Dioxide performs a number of vital functions in the human body including:

- Offloading of O_2 from the blood to be used by the cells.

- The dilation of the smooth muscle walls of the airways and blood vessels.

- The regulation of blood pH.[69]

---

68   Ibid, 26.
69   Ibid, 27.

He quotes Danish physiologist Christian Bohr, father of Nobel Prize-winning physicist Niels Bohr: "The CO_2 pressure of the blood is to be regarded as an important factor in the inner respiratory metabolism. If one used CO_2 in appropriate amounts, the oxygen that was taken up can be used more effectively throughout the body." McKeown summarizes, "The crucial point to remember is that O2 is released from the blood *when in the presence of* CO_2."[70] As we slow down our breathing, we increase the amount of CO2 in the blood to help the body more efficiently use O_2.

I appreciate the passion and commitment McKeown has brought to his study of breath. Faced with personal challenges, he worked to discover how he could improve his own life experience and then dedicated himself to sharing that knowledge for the benefit of others.

The invitation in this chapter was to step into the moment and begin by noticing your breath. You don't have to become an expert like McKeown, but you can take some simple action to improve your own life. What is exciting about the breath work is it can potentially change your life for the better. "Breathing at a specific and individualized (slow) breathing rate, termed resonance frequency (RF), where oscillations in heart rate (HR) and breathing synchronize" has shown through clinical research to provide numerous benefits, including:[71]

---

70   Ibid.

71   Jeffrey Pagaduan et al., "Acute effects of resonance frequency breathing on cardiovascular regulation," *Physiological Reports* 7, no. 2 (November 2019).

- Enhanced performance and reduced stress and anxiety[72]
- Positive influence on clinical symptoms in a number of disorders, including:
  - Depression[73]
  - Asthma[74]
  - Prehypertension[75]

- Reduced systolic blood pressure[76]
- Higher positive mood[77]
- Decreased pain and depressive symptoms for fibromyalgia patients[78]
- Diaphragm and stress reduction if needed[79]

---

72 Dylan J Jester et al., "Heart rate variability biofeedback: Implications for cognitive and psychiatric effects in older adults," *Aging & Mental Health* 23, 5 (2019): 574–580.

73 I. Mei Lin et al., "Heart rate variability biofeedback increased autonomic activation and improved symptoms of depression and insomnia among patients with major depression disorder," *Clinical Psychopharmacology and Neuroscience* 17, 2 (2019): 222–232.

74 Niloofar Taghizadeh et al., "Protective effect of heart rate variability biofeedback on stress-induced lung function impairment in asthma." *Respiratory Physiology & Neurobiology* 262 (April 2019): Pages 49-56.

75 Guiping Lin, "Heart rate variability biofeedback decreases blood pressure in prehypertensive subjects by improving autonomic function and baroreflex." *Journal of Alternative and Complementary Medicine* 18,2 (2010): 143–152.

76 Jeffrey Pagaduan et al., "Acute effects of resonance frequency breathing on cardiovascular regulation," *Physiological Reports* 7, no. 2 (November 2019).

77 Patrick R. Steffen et al., "The Impact of Resonance Frequency Breathing on Measures of Heart Rate Variability, Blood Pressure, and Mood," *Frontiers in Public Health,* 5 (2017).

78 Alex Zautra et al., "The effects of slow breathing on affective responses to pain stimuli: An experimental study," *Pain, 149, 1 (2010): 12-18.*

79 Xiao Ma et al., "The Effect of Diaphragmatic Breathing on Attention, Negative Affect and Stress in Healthy Adults," *Frontiers in Psychology,* 8 (2017).

Given the promising results, research is almost assuredly going to continue to explore the beneficial effects of conscious breathing. During a conversation with my colleague, Mikael, about the simple act of breathing, I discovered he and his officemates had a biweekly breathing practice. A former coworker had offered to guide everyone in the office for a breathing practice she would guide them through for twenty minutes twice weekly. Most didn't take it very seriously at first, but she persisted, and the positive results became tangible.

Now the entire office blocks off those twenty minutes to ensure they can attend, because they are feeling more calm and relaxed—even the executives are joining. When the original breathing teacher left for a new job, Mikael offered to become the new breathing guide. He told me during a recent work trip he was relieved (and practiced some deep diaphragmatic breathing to help him reduce his stress) to have found someone to take over his breathing guidance while he was away because this breathing practice has become so important to the weekly activities in his office.

Mikael wasn't trained as a doctor and never studied medicine, physiology, or kinesthesiology and has no formal training in yoga or breathing practices. He experienced the benefits of the practice, learned from his colleague, and now can share the experience with others. A clear example of how a simple practice can blossom into a life-changer.

Where is your breath?

CHAPTER SUMMARY

Our breath is always there with us, happening without a conscious thought, and we can also control it. We can moderate the pace, the depth, where we inhale, where we exhale, or how long we hold it. It can also bring us into the present moment as we feel the experience of our body breathing and our breath gently traveling in and out. Not only does it sustain life, but it also holds the key to well-being. Please keep feeling your breath as we move into listening with our bodies next.

CHAPTER SIX

TRY LISTENING FOR A CHANGE

———

Soughing. It has been my favorite word for a long time. According to Oxford, it is, "(of the wind in trees, the sea, etc.) to make a moaning, whistling, or rushing sound.

*We pushed off from the shore and glided into the heart of the river—around us just the sound of the wind **soughing** in the reeds and the lapping of water against the hull."*[80]

Not only does it describe a beautiful experience, but as a word, it just sounds cool to me. Back in the pine trees during my childhood family picnics, I liked to think of soughing as the trees speaking to me. The word alone is enough to take me to any number of wooded hikes I have had the pleasure to enjoy, either as guide or participant. For me, it is a pure form of listening with my ears, takes me deeply into my body, and reminds me of how I can create meaning from my listening.

---

80 *Lexico powered by Oxford.* s.v. "sough," accessed April 26, 2020.

My true paradigm shift in listening happened in 2010 thanks to my teacher, Bob Dunham (I've previously mentioned Bob's book *The Innovator's Way*). I was in Bob's Institute for Generative Leadership seeking to become a better leader, a more connected manager, and generally a better person.[81] Bob is a gifted teacher and student. He is full of great experiences he eloquently shares, learning practices with measures to assess progress and improvement, and a deep commitment to the rigor of his work and research.

It was his work on listening with which I most deeply connected, and I formed a fundamental practice in all of my conversations. I think it touched me so deeply because it was unspoken knowledge I already possessed. Bob magically brought it to life for me.

My most impactful teachers have shown me the way to learn, provided the guidance and support to sustain my learning, and maintained an objective perspective and measure on my progress. These teachers have enabled my transformational learning by helping me tap into some innate wisdom or truth I already had within that they helped me to rediscover and bring forth.

I have been told I am, and do consider myself, an excellent listener. Shy and introverted as a child, I was most comfortable listening to others. Fortunately, my brother did like to speak, so I was afforded the chance to practice listening. Thanks, brother—it was a gift that I got to practice listening!

---

81 "A Unique Framework for Elevating Your Leadership and Coaching Impact," Institute for Generative Leadership, accessed April 26, 2020.

Lacking confidence and uncomfortable speaking up or becoming the center of attention, listening provided me a way out of my discomfort. But as a child, this way out was only temporary relief. I would fill the time with thoughts of how I could contribute, how I could say something clever or be connected to the conversation. I took myself out of those moments of discomfort by filling my head with ideas of what could be. Sometimes long inner monologues would carry me far away and make me even more disconnected. I suspect this experience is familiar to some of you.

Anyway, in fifth grade, my teacher dedicated a portion of class for challenging his knowledge and intellect. We students would submit a question and he would attempt to answer it in front of the entire class. I think this was a fun exercise for most, but I do remember having a terrible experience with it. I believe the terribleness was magnified because I was busy in my head congratulating myself with my awesome question and clever answer that stumped the teach.

Well, I didn't stump him, or at least he didn't admit I did. After sharing my "stumper" it felt like I was being ridiculed by him for my explanation of my question and answer. He did this in front of the entire class. It was a terrible feeling: straight to my gut, shortness of breath, heart beating wildly, tingly all over, beet red face, elevated temperature. My body went into survival mode and froze. Others might have fought, and others might have run out in flight. Instead, it was my biological response to a perceived threat that caused me to freeze in that situation.

As I reflect and write about the experience now, I know it was clearly not a life-threatening situation, but my limbic and biological systems still felt it as a threat and responded as if the saber-toothed tiger was stalking me. The freeze response is not as well known as fight or flight, but there are clear examples of other animals responding this way.[82]

Even if we are not aware of it, listening is done with the full body. As we process sensory perception and the words we are hearing, we can begin to practice observing the feelings in our bodies and how our biology is responding. Bob helped me bring this understanding into conscious awareness.

In our listening, we are constantly making assessments, and if we are present when listening to others, we can assess their levels of commitment and trustworthiness and the serious-ness of offers and requests. This kind of listening is hap-pening on some level regardless of our awareness of it, so why not use that moment more efficiently? Think of all the miscommunication that might get cleared up with deeper, practiced listening in the present moment.

Now, what does listening feel like for me? Let's start with what it is not. When I am not present, I am often in my head, asso-ciating with a thought train reliving the past or fantasizing about the future. Not feeling sensation, but rather captive to my emotions. This is a state of reactivity, rather than creativity.

When I am present, I'm down in my body, not my head, and more empowered to actually take action. I am deeper in my body, feeling my support, and less excitable. From this place

---

82   Barry H. Hirst, "Secretin and the exposition of hormonal control," *Jour-nal of Physiology* 560, part 2 (October 2015): 339.

of presence, I can begin to feel the connection with others. As I feel into listening, I am more woven into the present moment. What is so rewarding about feeling into the listening and being present in the moment with another is that from this feeling state, I can feel the connection or disconnection and really assess the veracity of someone else's statements.

My fifth grade freeze response started in my gut, so let's explore this gut thing a bit more. Back on January 16, 1902, at University College London (UCL), William Bayliss and Ernest Henry Starling conducted an experiment leading to the discovery of the first hormone, secretin. By 1905, Starling shared his theories about hormones and functional control of the body at four Croonian Lectures to the Royal College of Physicians, during which he described chemical messengers which "have to be carried from the organ where they are produced to the organ which they affect by means of the bloodstream."[83]

We've known about the gut's power to influence our bodies for a long time, but until 2018, we only thought the gut communicated with our brain through hormones. It turns out that nerve cells in our gut are physically connected to our brain stem via the vagus nerve.[84] So rather than take minutes for hormones released by our gut to travel through our bloodstream to reach our brains, we have a nerve expressway from our gut to our brain that takes less than the blink of an eye to deliver a signal.[85]

---

83 Barry H. Hirst, "Secretin and the exposition of hormonal control," *Journal of Physiology* 560, part 2 (October 2015): 339.

84 Melanie Maya Kaelberer et al., "A gut-brain neural circuit for nutrient sensory transduction," *Science* 361, 6408 (September 18).

85 Emily Underwood, "Your gut is directly connected to your brain, by a newly discovered neuron circuit," *Science Magazine,* September 20, 2018.

I don't have the capacity to deeply explore the vagus nerve in this book, but I want to call your attention to it and plant the seed for further exploration in the future. My gut tells me there is a lot to unpack. Here are a couple of noteworthy facts:

- The vagus nerve is particularly well positioned to interface the immune and central nervous systems, and the vagus nerve has motor functions in the larynx, diaphragm, stomach, and heart and sensory functions in the ears, tongue, and visceral organs, including the liver.[86]

- The vagus nerve communicates arousing information from both favorable events, including a meal or deep breaths,[87] and aversive events, such as stress or inflammation.[88]

Let's try a practice for listening with your body in the moment. I invite you to pick a favorite song. It is important to have one with words and ideally one with words you know. Through familiarity, it is likely you've internalized some of the words. Listen through speakers, not earbuds nor a headset if possible, and try to do this alone for the freedom to really listen.

---

86 Christopher J Czura et al., "Cholinergic Regulation of Inflammation," in *Psychoneuroimmunology 4th edition*, ed. Robert Ader (Academic Press, 2007).

87 Michael W. Schwartz et al., "Central nervous system control of food intake," *Nature* 404 (2000): 661-671.

88 Seth A. Hayes et al., "Targeting Plasticity with Vagus Nerve Stimulation to Treat Neurological Disease," *Progress in Brain Research* 207 (2013): 275-299.

But DO NOT listen to the words. I repeat, DO NOT listen to the words (no offense to all the amazing lyricists out there).

As the music begins, find your favorite instrument in the music, rhythm, or lead. It doesn't matter. If that instrument is a human voice, don't focus on the words, but instead on the tonal quality of the voice. Follow the instrument with your body and feel the song. Really feel the song by sensing the music of that instrument. Now take a moment to find your breath and see if you can take a deep inhale into your belly to feel your lower ribs expand.

How about your jaw? Any clenching there?

Back to the instruments. Maybe mix it up and listen for a different instrument. Any change of your full-body listening? Where is the song taking you within your body? What are you feeling? This practice should be fun, so have fun with it. Repeat as often as you can with the same song or mix it up with different songs.

I find this to be a great practice for feeling into my body. For me, this practice is natural, as I default to listening to instruments—typically guitar, violin, Hammond B3 organ, or the human voice—without focusing on the words, and I don't "think" about the song except when my thought train rolls on, triggered by something—which can happen a lot. Find your breath, and feel that instrument again. Remember, this is a practice.

Now let's connect this practice to conversations.

Have you ever been in conversation with someone and found their attention to be elsewhere? They may be listening to conversations others are having and even jump into that other conversation rather than engage with you. They may be looking at their phone or looking for someone else in the room. I find this feels uncomfortable, really unsatisfying, and very disrespectful. Maybe I am incredibly boring or unsatisfying for them, but that discomfort I feel usually makes me want to shut down or keep the conversation at a transactional level—this for that.

What I am learning is that these feelings can help me take engagement to the next level. As I'm feeling their disconnect, I can work to reconnect. Seeking this reconnection is why getting familiar with my body can be so transformative. I can use the feelings in my body to help guide me into a deeper connection. These feelings are a window into the current state of others and provide new choices for me. This connection is not easy, either. Words can easily throw me out of the present and into a story of my own. When this happens, I notice my breath and feel that discomfort and explore what would feel better. I can take new actions from this place.

Where's your breath?

Another practice I liked to include back when I was teaching yoga was bringing atypical "meditation music" to play in class. I love the Grateful Dead and would play live albums to the class to try and help my students listen to their bodies in new ways. I made sure no one had an aversion to the Dead, but as long as they were open to it, I'd turn up the tunes. I found through my own practice that listening this way took me into my body differently, as I was listening with my body differently. My body was moving in a different way because of the music.

I wanted those who didn't listen to the Dead regularly to experience their yoga practice in a different way. It didn't need to be buttoned up in some silent practice; it could also be inspired and moved by music not designed for yoga. With breath and music, I was interested in playing with ways to get my students more into their bodies and more into their present moments. Different music also opened up the possibilities of taking their practice off the mat or into informal settings, a concept we will explore more in the final section of the book.

Can you feel into ways that you might listen differently? Areas of your body you might use besides your ears to understand what someone is actually saying?

CHAPTER SUMMARY
Listening can be a full body experience and biological studies show us our bodies are designed to listen with more than our ears; yet, it is really hard to do, so practicing listening with our bodies by feeling music can be a simpler way to begin. As we start to listen more deeply and feel what others are saying, we can change the dynamic of our conversations and begin to move into greater possibility. Listening with our bodies can bring us more fully into the present moment and help us become more capable of making new choices. Go grab something to chew on, because our next simple act is all about the power of chewing.

CHAPTER SEVEN

CHEW YOUR FOOD

——

"Chew your food!" You may have heard this phrase as a child or even as an adult. It is probably something you don't think much about and most likely don't do consciously. I sure didn't and often still don't. I can sometimes "inhale" my food, unconsciously consuming. What I have found is by bringing my attention to the chewing of my food, and actually counting the number of chews I take, I now have a completely new ritual to practice that brings me into my body and into the present moment and improves my overall well-being.

For years now, I have had a simple ritual in which I put a small offering of my meal to the side of my plate in thanks and appreciation. My brother and wife love this ritual, because when the meal is really good, they get an extra tasty bite. When dining with others, I typically do this in a very subtle and unobtrusive way, as it is a simple way for me to give thanks for the food and those that grew, harvested, prepared, and served it—taking a moment for all the lives that touched my meal.

This ritual of making an offering has brought consciousness and awareness into my experience of eating, or at least the moment before I eat. All too often, though, after making my offering, I will default into devouring my food, which is a relatively new phenomenon for me. I think I wait until I'm too hungry and need to "fill that hole quickly," so this is an area where I have more work to do.

My momma is an amazing cook, and as children, we had a home-cooked meal almost every night. Back then, I was a really slow eater. I mean really slow—I would still be eating after my family had left the table. Now as I said, these meals were delicious (still are—thanks, Momma!) so I wasn't avoiding eating. I was just taking my time.

One of my childhood family nicknames was the "Food Dude." I was the kid who was asking about dinner as we were sitting down for lunch or asking about the plans for dinner later in the week. I certainly had and still do have some peculiar food dislikes, but I really loved eating and was fortunate to never go hungry (remember privileged white boy, surrounded by love and the feeling of opportunity).

Within the last couple of years, I started noticing slight stomach discomfort when eating or shortly after eating. I was also eating too much because I was eating too quickly for my body's hormones to signal I was actually full. My eating pace meant I was swallowing too much air with each bite, and at times would be forced to take a break until the discomfort passed.

I found carbonated water helpful to relieve the pressure and it became a crutch during mealtimes. After committing to writing a book and discovering it was going to be about simple acts, the simple act of chewing surfaced as one of the practices I needed to share and practice myself. Chewing is very simple and hopefully something we can do many, many times per day. Inquiring into the simple act of chewing, I had an amazing flashback to 2005.

It was the weekend of December ninth, and I was living in New York City. On a cold morning with temperatures below freezing, I bundled up and hustled off to the Jazz at Lincoln Center's Frederick P. Rose Hall in the Time Warner Center at Columbus Circle. This session was going to be my second at the Institute for Integrative Nutrition (IIN).[89] The IIN was structured around primary learning from experts and practitioners sharing their perspectives and experience over a weekend. Hundreds of students from all over the country would travel to New York City approximately once a month for ten months.

We were supported to read and listen to leading nutritional theorists from across the spectrum—from vegan to Atkins and everything in between—and then experiment and practice on the weeks between classes with an approach and feel how it worked. Every weekend, there was a great lineup of experts; however, that particular weekend included someone I wasn't familiar with and wasn't really all that excited to hear from. Here is how the school previewed his talk in the preparatory email:

---

89 "About Us," Institute for Integrative Nutrition, Accessed April 25, 2020.

Lino Stanchich, teacher of the basic yet powerful art of how to eat as well as what, where, why, and when to eat. Author of Power Eating Program, Lino emphasizes the act of chewing of daily food for better health, mental clarity, fulfilling relationships, and spiritual development.

I thought to myself, *Really? Chewing? Chewing for better health, mental clarity, fulfilling relationships, and spiritual development?* At the time, I was more interested in Marion Nestle and her take on Food Politics[90] and Dr. Neal Barnard's perspective on veganism.[91] And yet it was Stanchich's talk I have come back to as I was struggling with my more recent stomach discomfort. It may have taken years for me to really connect with chewing and Stanchich's work, but it finally hit home. I'm so grateful the process of writing this book has helped me to deepen my experience of eating.

There were about five hundred students sitting in the Rose Auditorium. This session was only our second time gathering for the IIN journey, and many students had traveled long distances. There was a palpable excitement and joy in the room, and because the acoustics in the theater were so good, I felt the energy more than I heard it.

In walked Stanchich. I was immediately struck by his composure and calm. He looked to be about six feet tall, lean, and very comfortable in his own body. He had sharp features,

---

90   Marion Nestle, *FOOD POLITICS: HOW THE FOOD INDUSTRY INFLUENCES NUTRITION AND HEALTH*, (University of California Press, 2003).

91   Neal Barnard, Physicians Committee for Responsible Medicine, Accessed April 25, 2020.

a bald head with an Eastern European accented voice that was strong, but not overpowering. As he began to speak, the energy in the room collected around his story.

In 1943 Greece, Lino Stanchich's father, Antonio, was captured by Germans and sent to a concentration camp. Like in all German concentration camps, the living conditions were inhumane. His father told him, "I was cold most of the time and hungry all of the time."[92] This camp was connected to a factory where his father was expected to work. Meals included a cup of chicory coffee and a slice of bread in the morning, and a bowl of soup for both lunch and dinner. The soups were mostly water with a few vegetables and maybe some grains. People were dying of starvation daily, and during the cold winters, death from exposure increased dramatically.

It was in this living hell Antonio made the discovery he would credit for saving his life. One day when he was given some cold water, he intuitively kept the water in his mouth to chew it before swallowing it. Not only did this warm the water, but he noticed it seemed to give him added energy. He started experimenting with chewing, and for him, the magic number was 150 chews per mouthful. His practice became a simple one he shared with his friends: place one tablespoon of food or water in your mouth and chew 150 times, counting each chew. Many thought he was crazy and ten to twenty chews were enough, but two of his friends joined him in the chewing sessions and compared notes.

---

92   Lino Stanchich, *Power Eating Program*, (Asheville: Healthy Products, Inc., 1989), 3.

In 1945, after two years in the concentration camp, Lino's dad was liberated. Of the thirty-one men originally captured with his dad and sent to the concentration camp, only three survived: Antonio and his two friends who practiced chewing. The entire audience was riveted. All that energy was completely focused on Lino's words and the story he was telling. This practice was much deeper than some of the nutrition theories I had signed up to learn.

Now, there are arguably many variables that contributed to Lino's father's survival. What I think is important is what he believed. Antonio practiced a simple act that he believed would save his life. An act we are all familiar with yet do mindlessly. In the crucible of his struggle to survive, Antonio elevated the common and the automatic to the sublime. And that practice has since passed on to me and countless others, proving the power of simple acts beyond just our own experience. For me, Stanchich's story was impactful that day in December of 2005, but it didn't provide an immediate return. The real impact occurred nearly fifteen years later as I began practicing counting my chews. For me, 150 chews are not realistic. For some food, I can comfortably get to twenty-five or thirty chews. For other things, I'm lucky to get to eleven.

The invitation to practice this simple act is to begin by bringing awareness to your chewing. Like with the breath, just noticing the feeling of chewing.

When I first put my awareness on my chewing, I was really shocked at how little I was chewing—two, maybe five times!

It was almost as if I was in a race to get the food swallowed. Even nearly choking on my food didn't really slow me down for long. However, with time spent focusing my awareness on my chewing, I found a new appreciation for my food, a new relationship with my food, and less discomfort from my eating.

It has now become a game for me to see how much I can break down my food BEFORE swallowing. This practice has helped me focus on the present bite and mouthful, rather than focusing on the next bite—another example of how the act of a simple practice can bring awareness, and therefore me, into the moment.

Physical digestion begins in the mouth. One need only think back to Pavlov's research of ringing bells and salivating dogs.[93] What I didn't realize is that Pavlov was studying saliva in dogs and happened upon the conditioned response. If you don't have a dog and haven't experienced the need to clean up their "drool" as their full food bowl is on the way, you have probably at least felt it yourself when that anticipated favorite treat is coming and your mouth starts "watering."

Saliva is an important part of the digestion process. Saliva helps to moisten dry food and convert food into more easily digestible bits. It begins breaking down some starches and fats.[94] This simple act of chewing is not only helpful for finding the present moment, but also helps your biological system.

---

93 *Encyclopaedia Britannica Online*, s.v. "Ivan Pavlov," accessed April 25, 2020.

94 AM Pederson et al., "Saliva and gastrointestinal functions of taste, mastication, swallowing and digestion," *Oral Diseases* 8, 3 (May 2020): 117-129.

Your saliva's work is made much easier if you actually chew your food and break your food down into smaller pieces.

This simple practice of counting my chews helps me to break down my experience into precious moments. As this practice is newer for me, I'm not as consistent with it as I could be. This is part of the dance of life. Opportunities and potential practices come into our awareness, and we connect and resonate with some and those can stay around for a while. Others will come and go quickly or fade away more slowly. My experience with this chewing practice is a good reminder for me of this dance. Fifteen years ago, this practice didn't stick, yet it remained in my inventory and I found it when I needed it.

Please be kind to yourself as you attempt any of these new practices. You may find one that really sings to you, or we may just be planting seeds that will germinate years from now.   Don't forget to ask, "for the sake of what."

CHAPTER SUMMARY

Chewing is an essential part of eating, so we can do it mindlessly. Yet others have consciously used chewing as the means to survival in the harshest of circumstances. I have used the counting of my chews to ease discomfort, eat more slowly, and eat less. Counting my chews brings me into my body to joyfully experience eating, and it has taken many years for me to integrate this simple act into my daily practice. Chew that last bite, because we are going to get up and start moving again as we explore the simple act of walking.

CHAPTER EIGHT

WALKING

Twenty-six bones connected and evolved in a way that separates us anatomically from all other mammals. Often neglected and overlooked, our feet are a true marvel. Due to a break in the fossil record, we don't have any evidence to support speculation as to why our ancestors diverged from other apes. All we have are the results. Sometime between seven and four million years ago (yes, those darn big numbers again), our ancestors began walking upright.

Even before the size of the brain increased, the skeleton shifted to support upright walking, also known as bipedalism. These changes included the head moving back over the spine, the hips forming a pronounced scoop to hold the upper body, and the big toe shifting to align with the other bones of the feet. This big toe shift is really important, as apes have an opposable big toe that enables grasping and supports tree climbing. An inline big toe enables bipedalism over long distances.

I'm a big fan of Carol Ward's work and theory that our ancestors evolved from something less like modern apes and chimps and more likely closer to our bipedal selves.[95] The combination of modern scientific approaches is creating a better picture of our ancestors and helping to bring the fossilized bones to life, deepening our hypothetical theories.

Another hero in the paleoanthropological world is Mary Leakey. Born in 1913, right in the middle of the special century, Leakey contributed to a series of significant discoveries expanding our understanding of human evolution. Back in 1976, she was leading a team on an archaeological expedition in Laetoli, Tanzania. PBS describes the scene like this:

> *Thank goodness for the irrepressible urge of humans (and other animals) to joke and play around in nearly any situation. Sometimes, it pays big dividends. It certainly did in 1976, when paleoanthropologist Andrew Hill and a colleague were tossing elephant dung at each other in Laetoli, a hominid archeological site in Tanzania. As Hill dived out of the way, he stumbled on what turned out to be one of the wonders of prehistoric finds: a trail of hominid footprints about 3.6 million years old.*
>
> *The majority of the Laetoli footprint site was excavated in 1978. Until then, the oldest known footprints of human ancestors were tens of thousands of years old. But this trail, some eighty feet long and preserved in cementlike volcanic ash, had been made by some of the first upright-walking hominids. An almost unimaginable sequence of events preserved what*

---

95 Carol Ward, "Unraveling the Mystery of Human Bipedality," interview by Tom Garlinghouse, *Sapiens* May 29, 2019.

paleontologist Ian Tattersall calls a fossil of human behavior—prehistoric walking.[96]

Amazing! Upright walking captured in stone from more than three million years ago.

Figure 1. Fidelis T Masao et al., "New footprints from Laetoli (Tanzania) provide evidence for marked body size variation in early hominins," eLife 5 (December 2016).

The early humans who left these prints were bipedal and had big toes in line with the rest of their foot, which means these early human feet were more human-like than ape-like, as apes have highly divergent big toes that help them climb and grasp material like a thumb does. The footprints also show that the gait of these early humans was "heel-strike" (the heel of the foot hits first) followed by "toe-off" (the toes push off at the end of the stride)—the way modern humans walk.[97]

---

96 "Laetoli Footprints," PBS Evolution Library, accessed April 26, 2020.

97 "Laetoli Footprint Trails," Smithsonian National Museum of Natural History, What does it mean to be human? accessed April 26, 2020.

Now, why all this science and history? It helps reinforce the fact we were designed to move and those of us who can walk should likely be walking more. But before we get into walking, let's start with standing. My favorite anatomy teacher, Amy Matthews, taught anatomy during my training with Jill Satterfield.[98] What a wonderful semester. Their wisdom, experience, and generosity were woven together to form the foundation of my embodied experience and practice.

They like to speak of the feet as triangles. The triangle is formed with one point under the mound (the meaty place under the joint at the base of the toe) of the big toe, one point under the mound of the little toe, and one point under the middle of the heel.

If you can, take a moment to prepare to stand in bare feet. I'm going to give some instructions for standing, so read through them, and then I invite you to put the book down and practice. Like everything in this book, the practices are an invitation and only you know what is right for your body. Only do what feels right and safe.

Stand up in bare feet and see if you can feel the triangles. In your right foot, shift your weight from front to back between those three points of the triangle. Now shift your weight from side to side in the right foot between those triangle points. Take the moment to notice anything that might have changed by experiencing the triangles and moving your weight within the right foot.

---

98 Amy Matthews, Embodied Asana, accessed April 26, 2020.

Now repeat those front-to-back and side-to-side shifts with your left foot. Take the moment to notice any changes in your experience with the left foot. What about any changes in your body as you moved from right to left foot? Do you notice any change in your physical self? Do you feel a tingling or pulsation, a temperature change, a shift in your sense of balance? How about feeling your bones and muscles in new ways? Maybe even some muscles you don't normally notice? Do you notice a change in your mood or feel any emotional change? Don't feel as if you need to experience any of these things. As always, the invitation is to just notice.

Many folks don't walk around barefoot much, so this may feel really strange. Strange can be good. After all, they are your feet. Most of us wrap our feet up in socks, then put on shoes that may or may not be helping or supporting our anatomy, and rush off to tend to the things on our list.

We jump into our heads and move through the day as a disembodied brain. Maybe we make it home at the end of our day worn out and exhausted, and as Mr. Burns from *The Simpsons* would say, "release the hounds." Those dogs are barking from shuffling us around on our daily adventure.

Maybe you can start tomorrow by connecting into the tri-angles of your feet as your feet hit the ground. If that doesn't work, maybe you can take a break during the day to feel them or when you get home from any activities that have filled your day and likely your head.

"You've got to be comfortable in your own company," says George Meegan,[99] Guinness World Record Holder for the fastest journey along the Pan-American highway on foot. Meegan "walked 30,431 kilometers (19,019 miles) in a journey that took him from the southernmost point of South America, at Ushuaia, Argentina, to the northernmost point of North America, at Prudhoe Bay in Alaska, USA, taking 2,426 days from 26 January 1977 to 18 September 1983."[100]

Meegan's sentiment is at the heart of this practice of simple acts. These simple acts of finding presence in the moment bring us closer to our true nature. Walking holds a special place in our practice of simple acts. Ferris Jabr wrote a great piece in *The New Yorker* about how walking helps us think.

> *When we go for a walk, the heart pumps faster, circulating more blood and oxygen, not just to the muscles but to all the organs—including the brain. Many experiments have shown that after or during exercise, even very mild exertion, people perform better on tests of memory and attention. Walking on a regular basis also promotes new connections between brain cells, staves off the usual withering of brain tissue that comes with age, increases the volume of the hippocampus (a brain region crucial for memory), and elevates levels of molecules that both stimulate*

99 Rose McLaughlin, *Meegan-A Short Documentary*, February 15, 2016, Video, 5:20.

100 "Fastest journey of the Pan-American highway on foot," Guinness World Record, accessed April 26, 2020.

the growth of new neurons and transmit messages between them.[101]

Walking has also been a documented practice for many geniuses:

> *From Aristotle instructing students while they meandered around to Charles Darwin's daily pacing of a path he had explicitly installed for thinking, to Silicon Valley heroes like Mark Zuckerberg and Steve Jobs who have sworn by walking meetings, a shockingly high percentage of great minds loved to wander.*[102]

By all means, use walking as a method to maintain your health, as inspiration for your creativity, or as a way to conduct more productive and efficient brainstorming meetings, *and* try using walking as a simple act to find the present moment. Jabr describes it beautifully,

> *Walking at our own pace creates an unadulterated feedback loop between the rhythm of our bodies and our mental state that we cannot experience as easily when we're jogging at the gym, steering a car, biking, or during any other kind of locomotion. When we stroll, the pace of our feet naturally vacillates with our moods...*[103]

---

101 Ferris Jabr, "Why Walking Helps Us Think," *New Yorker*, September 3, 2014.

102 Jessica Stillman, "The Simple Trick Great Thinkers From Charles Darwin to Steve Jobs Used to Be More Creative," *Inc.,* accessed April 26, 2020.

103 Ferris Jabr, "Why Walking Helps Us Think," *New Yorker*, September 3, 2014.

I invite you to find a place you can focus completely on your walking, a safe environment where you have fewer distractions to grab your attention. Maybe in a hallway or in a small room where you can walk in circles, or you can even try walking in place. We are going to fully focus on the sensation of walking and the feeling of our feet moving through the act of walking. Try it barefoot so you can feel your feet directly on the ground or floor.

Before you begin, take a moment to notice where you feel your breath. Make an assessment of how you feel or what your mood is. As you begin, notice the sensation of your feet on the ground and the feeling of the weight transition through one foot and then transfer to the other. Notice how your feet connect to the ground as you move through the motion.

Are you walking like our ancestors on a plain in Tanzania—heel-strike to toe-off?

Can you vary how your feet connect and touch the ground in your practice?

Can you move through the movement so slowly you can feel each inch of your foot touching upon the ground before lifting off?

If you pick up your pace, do you lose the connection to your feet and the ground?

What does it take to get back to that moment of sensation on the ground?

Can you take a moment as you are walking and give thanks for the fact that you can walk? There are plenty of people who cannot walk or cannot walk unassisted; maybe you can dedicate this walking practice to them.

CHAPTER SUMMARY

Walking is our history. It differentiates us from all other life on Earth. It can also be more than the means to get from place to place. Remember, these bodies of ours are not just vehicles for moving our thoughts around—they help us take action in the world. Start by bringing your awareness to the act of standing before moving into walking. Feel your feet and shift your weight around. Begin to recognize the nuances in just standing and cultivate your skill in noticing your connection to the Earth. Walking is good for our health, our brains, and our creativity, and it is a simple act that can connect us with the present moment and more deeply with the earth. Walking can also help carry us over to that blooming gardenia plant to more deeply inhale that magical aroma, so get ready as we move into our noses and explore smell in the next chapter.

CHAPTER NINE

I SMELL THAT

———

The old adage says to stop and smell the roses. I invite you to take this moment to notice what you smell. For me, odors are often in the background without my taking much conscious notice. Strong or unpleasant smells seem to grab my attention more easily, and there are those smells that can transport me directly back into the past. Yet often odors are impacting me without my noticing. Awareness of odors feels even more important now that a symptom of COVID-19 is losing the ability to smell. So now, practicing noticing what we smell, and more importantly if we *can't* smell, might lead to an early identification of infection.

> *"Based on our study, if you have smell and taste loss, you are more than ten times more likely to have COVID-19 infection than other causes of infection. The most common first sign of a COVID-19 infection remains fever, but fatigue and loss of smell and taste follow as other very common initial symptoms." said*

Carol Yan, MD, an otolaryngologist and head and neck surgeon at UC San Diego Health.[104]

Smells are a powerful trigger for our memories. Like a time machine, smells can take us out of the present and straight into the past. Managed by our olfactory system, these smells can unlock memories that can influence the actions and the choices we have in the present moment. "Olfactory nerves transmit the sensation of smell to the brain."[105] As smells enter the nose, they create signals for the olfactory bulb, which then signals two places within the brain: smell identification in the olfactory cortex, and the limbic system, associated with emotion, behavior, and memory storage.[106]

Of particular interest is the power smells have on our auto-biographical memories (AMs), two types of memories: "personal semantic information (i.e., facts about the self, such as knowing where one was born) and personal episodic information (i.e., unique events, such as remembering a first day of school)."[107]

Evidence shows that olfactory evoked personal information is different from information evoked by the primary senses. Of note:

104 University of California - San Diego, "Loss of smell and taste validated as COVID-19 symptoms in patients with high recovery rate: Study suggests clinicians should include sensory impairment as standard screening measure," *ScienceDaily*, April 13, 2020.

105 David Myland Kaufman, *Clinical Neurology for Psychiatrists, Chapter 4 Cranial Nerve Impairments*, (Elsevier, 2007), 27.

106 Ibid.

107 Alisha C. Holland et al., "Emotion and Autobiographical Memory," *Physics of Life Review*, 7, no. 1 (Mar 2010): 88-131.

- *Distinct AMs involving olfactory information are formed earlier in life than those comprising verbal and visual information. This observation supports research showing that associative odor learning begins very early in life.*
- *Odor-evoked AMs are accompanied by stronger feelings of being brought back in time to the occurrence of the events.*
- *Given that the olfactory nerves project directly to the amygdala complex, it has been proposed that odor-evoked AM are more emotional than memories cued by other modalities. Indeed, most studies suggest an emotional advantage of olfactory evoked AMs over verbally and visually evoked memories.[108]*

Since smell can so strongly trigger emotions and emotional memories, it is not surprising:

> *The global perfume market size was valued at USD 31.4 billion in 2018 and is expected to expand at a CAGR [compound annual growth rate] of 3.9 percent from 2019 to 2025. The market growth is attributed to growing trend of personal grooming, coupled with increasing demand for luxury and exotic fragrances. Moreover, increasing consumer spending on premium and luxury fragrances due to high income level, along with improving living standards, is driving the global market. In recent years, perfumes have evolved into*

---

108 Maria Larsson et al., "Olfactory LOVER: behavioral and neural correlates of autobiographical odor memory," *Frontiers in Psychology*, 5, no. 312 (April 11, 2014).

a significant business in the cosmetics and personal care industry. Perfumes have emerged as an essential product driven by the growing trend of personal care, forming a part of pride and confidence.[109]

With disposable income, we can act on the desire to surround ourselves with pleasant smells and ideally create positive memories. We come by it naturally, as evidence points to perfume and scents as a part of the daily routine and ritual in the lives of the ancient Egyptians, Romans, Greeks, and Chinese.[110] In 2007, archaeologists announced, "The world's oldest perfumes have been found on Cyprus. The world's oldest perfumes were scented with extracts of lavender, bay, rosemary, pine, or coriander and kept in tiny translucent alabaster bottles. The remaining traces found in Pyrgos, on the south of the island, are more than 4,000 years old."[111]

My first memory of perfume factories comes from Tom Robbins's classic *Jitterbug Perfume*,[112] and the LeFever brothers' misadventures. As I was writing this chapter at the Charleston Public Library John's Island branch, I was ecstatic to find the library had a copy. After finding the copy in the fiction section, I opened it, took an inhale, and was transported back to elementary school and reading

---

109 Grand View Research, Perfume Market Size, Share & Trends Analysis Report By Product (Mass, Premium), By End User (Men, Women), By Distribution Channel (Offline, Online), By Region, And Segment Forecasts, 2019 - 2025, (Jun 2019) Accessed April 26, 2020.

110 JR Thorpe, "The Strange History Of Perfume, From Ancient Roman Foot Fragrance To Napoleon's Cologne," *Bustle*, July 31, 2015.

111 Malcom Moore, "Eau de BC: the oldest perfume in the world," *The Telegraph*, March 21, 2007.

112 Tom Robbins, *Jitterbug Perfume*, (New York: Bantam Books, 1990).

The Book of Three[113] by Lloyd Alexander—my earliest days of science fiction fantasy adventure. That smell is deeply satisfying. I feel safe and cared for, ready to embark on an adventure, and always grateful for the love, opportunity, and privilege I have been given.

What is tricky about scent and our sense of smell is that it is so directly wired into our brains that it's hard for me to really feel the moment. Smelling a book almost immediately transports me back in time and connects to memories. If you are reading this in a hardback or paperback version, I invite you to take an inhale of the book and see what happens. If you are using an e-reader or listening to an audio version, just take an inhale to see what you might notice and smell. Can you experience the momentary feeling of the smell before being transported back in time? Become aware of any kind of emotion or feeling that arises through this experience. Now become aware that those feelings or emotions are present in this moment and affecting this experience. Remember smell can be affecting you subtly throughout your day.

It is important to understand that smell is a very subjective sense. Compared to me, my wife has a very strong sense of smell. It is a running joke between us about how bad something must smell for me to smell it. Don't assume others can smell what you can. A science team lead by Noam Sobel at the Weizmann Institute of Science has attempted to better understand:

---

113 Lloyd Alexander, *The Book of Three*, (New York: Henry Holt and Company, 1964).

Whether people are similar or different in their olfactory perception. This question, however, must be answered with caution, even with the current data in hand. If we look at gross olfactory perception, people remain quite similar to one another. If we take the average perception of an odor, it serves as a reasonable estimation of what any given individual will say about that odor. However, once we applied the method we developed for maximizing differences, we find that olfactory perception was highly individually specific and variable across individuals.

Incredibly, they found through extrapolating from the data and using enough odors and descriptors they could "fingerprint" or individually identify each of the seven billion people on Earth,[114] another indicator of our individual uniqueness with our DNA programming processing experiences in our own special ways. With our noses, each of us is experiencing the world in our own unique way.

According to astronaut Don Pettit, even space has a smell. As Pettit put it:

I had the pleasure of operating the airlock for two of my crewmates while they went on several space walks. Each time, when I repressed the airlock, opened the hatch and welcomed two tired workers inside, a peculiar odor tickled my olfactory senses. At first, I couldn't quite place it. It must have come from the air ducts

---

114 Lavi Secundo et al., "Individual olfactory perception reveals meaningful nonolfactory genetic information," *Proceedings of the National Academy of Science*, 112, no. 28 (Jul 2015): 8750-8755.

that re-pressed the compartment. Then I noticed that this smell was on their suit, helmet, gloves, and tools. It was more pronounced on fabrics than on metal or plastic surfaces. It is hard to describe this smell; it is definitely not the olfactory equivalent to describing the palette sensations of some new food as "tastes like chicken." The best description I can come up with is metallic; a rather pleasant sweet metallic sensation. It reminded me of my college summers where I labored for many hours with an arc welding torch repairing heavy equipment for a small logging outfit. It reminded me of pleasant sweet-smelling welding fumes. That is the smell of space.[115]

Back on Earth, when I was teaching yoga, I liked to bring essential oils or plant extracts into class to help generate a positive feeling and mood in the room. For some, the effect was obvious, and for others, I'm not sure they ever noticed a big shift. I would always ask if people had any allergies or objections I should be concerned about before sharing a certain scent because I never wanted to create a negative reaction.

At times, I would even integrate therapeutic-grade essential oil of peppermint into the practice of the class. I found peppermint oil was enlivening and brought a positive energy into the room. If a student was willing, I would offer them some peppermint oil on their skin over a muscle or part of their body that was bothering or aggravating them. The smell of

---

115 Don Pettit, "The Smell of Space," Expedition Six Space Chronicles #4, Accessed April 26, 2020.

the peppermint picked up their energy and brought a strong tingling sensation to their skin. The warming and tingling of the peppermint oil helped keep their awareness on the spot bothering them for a good part of the ninety-minute class. This awareness enabled them to work with that spot in multiple positions and potentially discover new ways of moving or relating to the body.

Vanilla essence and coffee extracts are often used to test the olfactory nerve, so you may want to start there: either smelling coffee or vanilla and ensure your nose is working. Then see where those scents take you. Are there any vivid memories those smells access for you? If so, what are the emotions and feelings associated with them?

When my friend Morgan was battling terminal cancer, she found certain blends of essential oils created a positive mood for her when she was going through some of her more difficult treatments. Through the worst of it, she remained positive and was an inspiration until her last day. She made essential oil blends to share with others, and when I smell her "Joyful Pony," I remember her smile, kindness, and that beautiful hike we did in the Shining Rock Wilderness.

If you are motivated, you might experiment by finding some smells that take you to your "happy place." Once you find one, see if you can keep it handy and available. If you are anticipating a difficult conversation, meeting, or event, apply that smell with positive associations before that conversation or event. It should support you and provide the confidence, calm, and generosity to more effectively connect and engage in that moment. This practice need not be extravagant, but it can be powerful.

CHAPTER SUMMARY

We are surrounded by scents and odors, and our sense of smell is wired directly into the part of our brain responsible for emotion, behavior, and memory storage. This connection makes the practice of working with scents as a way into the present moment so tricky. Since scents are tied to memories and emotions, we can be sent to our past or generate an emotion that might be incongruent with the present moment before a full breath is complete. Further complicating matters is that everyone has their own unique olfactory profile, so scent-related experiences are very subjective. The opportunity to practice observing scents in an experimental way can help us to discover what is already happening and get empowered to navigate unexpected emotional responses or better support ourselves in challenging circumstances. We are now prepared to begin integrating these simple acts more deeply into our daily lives.

SECTION THREE

CHAPTER TEN

INFORMAL PRACTICE

———

These simple acts we've been discussing, and hopefully you have been practicing, are with you for the rest of your life. They are fundamental. Because they are fundamental and you are already doing them, I have been inviting you to bring more awareness into them. Do them more consciously. As we bring more consciousness into these simple acts, it taps us into the present moment. When we're in the present moment, we can access our superpower of options. Given the state of the world and the broken systems all around, we need resilience, and options support our resilience.

My dad has continually impressed upon my brother and me that "it is all about options." Now, as a well-educated white male born in the United States in the twentieth century, I have won the lottery of options. I recognize the options I have are very different than those for any minority born to similar circumstances. I understand the structural mechanisms that separate and divide us as humans, advantage some at the cost of others, threaten countless lives through the tragic consequences of environmental devastation; hell, even the consequences from the current pandemic sparked by COVID-19 won't change with a single breath or conscious chew. However, I remain optimistic and hopeful these simple acts can become the beginning of the journey we can all share together to fix these problems.

I am arguing that we must be fully "in our bodies" and present in the moment to connect and collaborate with others on any of the challenges we face, both as people and societies. I have faith when we are connecting as humans, we **will** collaboratively solve society's problems. I understand being in the present moment and fully "in our bodies" is scary and even terribly painful for some. We have built industries to help us avoid the present moment and provide quick fixes to the physical pain we experience.

I began this conversation back in the introduction, describing that these simple acts were not easy, just simple. They are simple in the sense that we are already doing them, hard in the fact that bringing our awareness into them takes practice. These practices have been offered as a way to feel into your own experience. Now we've shared these fundamental practices, the next offer I would like to share is integrating these practices into your daily experience, expanding the places in which to practice.

One of the many things we are not taught as children, or at least I was not taught, is how the body actually works. Imagine if, in gym class, beyond just playing games and burning energy, we learned how to properly engage our core, or maybe even what our core actually is and how it works. Imagine if we learned about pelvic tilt and how many muscles are used to rotate and extend our shoulders.

I think as a child I didn't appreciate or respect my body much. I don't think I even thought about it, so maybe these kinds of lessons wouldn't stick when we are kids. Maybe as children, our bodies are just more resilient, but by the time I was in my thirties, my body was telling me things I didn't understand.

Any feeling sense—tickle, tingle, heat or cold, ache and pain, heartburn, fever, _____ (you fill in the blank)— is our body speaking to us, rather than with us, too often because we just don't have the ability to understand what it's saying. In my thirties, I knew I needed to learn more about my body and what it was trying to tell me. I chose to begin my journey into learning about my body through embodiment practices to better understand it and what it was trying to tell me.

One of the big challenges I had with many embodiment practices was they compartmentalized the practice. There was a separation between the practice and everyday life. This isn't very surprising because life typically gets compartmentalized.

This is work time.

This is play time.

This is family time.

This is solo time.

And yet, the wisdom from any embodiment practice can inform every moment of our lives. Without its conscious integration, the power of learning is squandered and minimized. Let's think about integrating these practices into all aspects of our lives as informal practice. Every time you chew is a chance to practice. Every time you listen to anyone speaking is a chance to practice. Every step you take is another chance to practice. Every breath you take provides a chance to practice.

My invitation is to bring this informal practice into the very mundane. How about when doing the dishes? I never liked doing the dishes. I was usually doing them after eating a delicious meal and didn't want to be literally immersed in the leftovers or the associated mess while digesting. I didn't like the feel of my hands during and particularly after doing the dishes. As satisfying as getting all the dishes clean can be, there were always things that required more effort to get clean than I thought necessary and that usually made me fussy.

One day I shifted that experience. Recall our definition of experience:

> *The sense of something you personally accomplish, something that you do to affect outcomes, or something that makes you feel a certain way (e.g., "I had a great time playing tennis").*[116]

I began doing the dishes with my feet. Not literally, but kinda. As I was standing there at the sink, I actually felt my feet and the support they were getting from the floor. I felt the way my connection to the floor changed as I shifted my weight about

---

116 J. Robert Rossman and Mathew D. Duerden, *Designing Experiences*, (Columbia University Press, 2019), Chapter One.

from foot to foot and front to back. I felt the front of my legs and hips bones touch against the sink itself and change their connections with my shifting weight.

I could shift my awareness into the sink, and the fork or plate I found myself cleaning, and attempt to return that utensil to its natural state before the meal was prepared, cooked, served, and eaten. I found I could shift my awareness of my hands away from any discomfort and into the action of the cleaning. Once those dishes were clean and either drying in the rack or hand-dried, the rewarding satisfaction from finishing was intensified by cleaning the dishes with a focus in the moment.

For me, that practice at the sink doing dishes remains one of shifting focus and awareness. That is a great place to be. Your awareness is moving throughout your body. As you do this more quickly, you start to approximate this feeling of an expanded awareness.

Let's explore this idea of expanded awareness a bit now.

I have found there are places that can be easier for me to expand my awareness. A personal favorite is to immerse myself in a natural setting. For me, a natural setting can open my awareness up as I feel an affinity and connection to the world around me. Since I was a child, I have always been called to trees. That soughing from an early age spoke to me. Not to climb them like my brother did, but to be among them. My life's journey hasn't always surrounded me with trees, but I feel a deep satisfaction with them. My spirits lifted; my awareness expanded.

I was recently on a hike with my wife in the Point Reyes National Seashore exploring some of the beaches there. We found a particularly secluded cove, and while we wanted to continue down the beach, the water was too high to get past. Since it still wasn't low tide, we decided to wait a bit and see what would happen. I ended up finding a comfortable spot on a rock to sit and feel my breath. It was hard! Warm in the sun and then chilly as the clouds obscured it. The irregular rhythm of the surf crashing and receding. The call of birds coming and going.

For me, just feeling my breath was hard in that setting. Yet I had moments of great expansiveness, too. It was so much harder to be just in my breath surrounded by a beautiful kaleidoscope of momentary experiences yet feel greater than my breath at the same time. Our lives can feel unmanageably busy and the complexity can feel overwhelming, but each moment can still be accessed through our bodies. Informal practice is important because it can help us integrate these simple acts into our daily lives. Few of us can go off to a cave for years at a time to go deep with this inquiry. Rather, we are afforded the opportunity to informally bring this practice into our everyday moments.

We didn't go any further on that hike because the water level never dropped enough for us to pass. Plus, the chill that had set in after the clouds thickened started to seep into my bones. We climbed up from the beach to find a place for lunch and came upon this regal eucalyptus tree. The clouds had moved on once again.

Figure 2. Kessler iPhone panoramic, National Seashore, February 2, 2020.

Such majesty and beauty. The epitome of resilience. We were honored to eat our lunch nearby. That meal from Inverness Park Market—kale Caesar salad and an Italian hero with the olive bites—all exploded with flavor as I deliberately chewed and deeply tasted that meal. I was very present.

Thanks to the COVID-19 pandemic, I don't know when I will make it back there. The disease has so dramatically altered life for all: taken far too many lives, too quickly and in great pain; brought deep suffering to countless families and friends mourning their loss; and forced entire industries closed and millions of people into unemployment, while we attempt to slow the spread of the disease. Social distancing a new norm, as the way we interact and connect with others has been radically changed. We have even managed to find a way for this deadly virus to deepen fault lines between people with differing ideologies and political views.

Given all of this, I invite you to try for thirty minutes outside surrounded by other living things that aren't humans within the next week. Take a month if you need it, but get outside.

Regardless of the month, go find yourself an ocean, a lake or pond, a river, a creek, or waterfall. Find a mountain range in the distance or all around you with trees, lots of trees, or maybe a barren area with just the wisp of life hanging on in tiny crags. Or maybe you find farmland or gardens, or well-groomed lawns like a city park.

For those who live in cities, landscape architects have given a generous gift. For urban dwellers (which more and more of us are becoming each year)[117] who can't travel to the wilderness, urban parks offer a perfect setting for this informal practice and efforts to expand awareness. While these parks have been designed by humans, they can still deliver an easier place for me to practice expanding my awareness.

However, I must be present with the moment to truly appreciate the gift. Having grown up outside of New York City and then living for nearly a decade near Central Park, I have deep admiration and appreciation for Frederick Law Olmsted, Sr., and his colleague Calvert Vaux who gave the city its greatest ongoing gifts, Central Park and Prospect Park. They were also the first to use the term landscape architect.[118] I had the good fortune to live in Asheville, North Carolina and join the membership of the Biltmore Estate to enjoy Olmsted's work on at least a weekly basis while living there.[119]

---

117 Global Health Observatory, "Urban Population Growth," World Health Organization, accessed May 24, 2020.

118 Charles Beveridge, "Frederick Law Olmsted Sr.," National Association for Olmsted Parks, accessed May 24, 2020.

119 "Grounds and Gardens," Biltmore Estate, accessed May 24, 2020.

In his work, "Olmsted believed that it was the purpose of his art to affect the emotions. This was especially evident in his park design, where he created passages of scenery in which the visitor would become immersed, experiencing the restorative action of the landscape by what Olmsted termed an 'unconscious' process. To achieve this result, he subordinated all elements of the design to the single purpose of making the landscape experience most profound."[120] I find the experience to be profound, as my awareness expands to feel as much as possible.

If you can find the time and space for informal practice, remember to set your intention. For the sake of what are you venturing into this green space? It turns out if you are aware of your needs, you can be intentional with your action in this urban green space. Walking is more favorable for stress reduction, and sitting in urban green space is better for attention restoration.[121] Like all the practices we've been exploring, this informal practice is also multidimensional. The benefits can be reduced stress or focused attention, and they can also serve as a way to expand your awareness and connect more deeply with the world around you.

For some, finding the time or the place for thirty minutes outside surrounded by non-human life might be impossible. Not enough time, no way to get there, mobility impairment—whatever the reason, sadly, this is the reality for some. While not a solution for everyone, studies into the benefits of virtual

120 Charles Beveridge, "Frederick Law Olmsted Sr.," National Association for Olmsted Parks, accessed May 24, 2020.

121 Wei Lin et al., "Sitting or Walking? Analyzing the Neural Emotional Indicators of Urban Green Space Behavior with Mobile EEG," *Journal of Urban Health* 97 (2020): 191–203.

reality (VR) immersion in natural settings appear to be promising. While a lot more work still needs to be done, nature experiences through VR could help bring the health benefits of the natural world to those who can't get there.[122]

Still, VR or not, I believe presence is the foundation for the experience. For now, as we wait on future studies of the possibilities of VR immersion, bringing audio recordings into any practice is worth experimenting with to see if and how the experience of the present moment changes. My friend Mikael from Chapter Five, who leads the breathing practice at work, brings bird and water sounds into the practice he leads for his colleagues. What can you do to bring new experiences to your present moment as you expand your awareness through informal practice?

CHAPTER SUMMARY

The simple acts we have been discussing, and you've hopefully been practicing, have been offered as a way to engage with your body and access the present moment. They are also practices you can integrate into your daily life through more informal exercise. Taking these simple acts into my daily life helps to support me by providing greater options, as I can feel the possibility from the moment. Getting into a natural setting or environment has helped me to feel a sense of expansiveness as I practice these simple acts. I hope you can find thirty minutes outside to feel your body in the natural world. In our next chapter, we are going explore the power of awe.

---

122 Matthew P. White et al., "A prescription for 'nature'–the potential of using virtual nature in therapeutics," *Neuropsychiatric Disease and Treatment* 14 (2018): 3001-3013.

CHAPTER ELEVEN

THE OVERVIEW EFFECT

———

Come on another journey with me. October 29, 1998: it is a cool and crisp day at the Kennedy Space Center in Florida. You are fortunate enough to be at Banana Creek, the VIP section, only 3.29 miles away from Launch Complex 39B. You recognize a voice over the crackling loudspeakers and hear:

"*T-minus 10*

9

8

we have a go for main engine start...

5

4

3

2

1

Booster ignition and lift off of Discovery with a crew of six astronaut heroes and one American legend."

Originally scheduled for two p.m., minor technical problems and a couple of overzealous observers in an aircraft flying into restricted air space to get a better look delayed liftoff until 2:19:34 in the afternoon. It is not uncommon for a rocket launch to be delayed. They are complex machines containing large, controlled explosions. There is a lot going on, so a slight delay is no big deal for safety.

The first thing I noticed after ignition is the exploding plumes of gray and white smoke against the pale blue sky. At 3.29 miles away, the crackling sounds of those controlled explosions quickly reached the ears, followed immediately by the low rumble I felt in my chest. My breath caught as my mind struggled with the feeling of that rumble. The growl ultimately spread to my entire body, which was hard to comprehend coming from a source so far away.

Oxford describes awe as "a feeling of reverential respect mixed with fear or wonder" and this was definitely awe.[123] Such a thing can commonly produce tears in those fortunate enough to *feel* a rocket launch.

Back on the space shuttle Discovery, the astronauts were accelerating from zero through 2.5 Gs up to about forty-five seconds, at which point the space shuttle's main engines were throttled back to reduce vehicle stress. Once through that period of maximum dynamic pressure, the engines are throttled back up, eventually pushing the crew through three Gs before main engine cut off about eight and a half minutes later.

They were now falling around the earth about 17,500 miles per hour. Payload Specialist John Glenn and his fellow crew

---

123 *Lexico powered by Oxford.* s.v. "awe," accessed April 26, 2020.

members, Commander Curtis L. Brown, Pilot Steven W. Lindsey, Mission Specialists Scott E. Parazynski, Stephen K. Robinson, and Pedro Duque, and Payload Specialist Chiaki Mukai were now in orbit, and Glenn had finally returned to space thirty-six years later.

I had heard that after John Glenn came back from his Friendship Seven mission, the first American to orbit the earth in 1962, President Kennedy refused to allow Glenn back into space because the country and the space program could not risk losing such an American hero. I don't know if it's actually true and never bothered to check, but I do know he was tenacious in his efforts to return to space, and I think the world of the Ohio senator.

From space, the astronauts described a shift in their perception of the planet. Astronaut Frank White wrote about it in his book, titled *The Overview Effect: Space Exploration and Human Evolution*.

> And what the astronauts were telling me was, I knew before I went into orbit, or went to the moon, that there weren't any little dotted lines (country borders). But it's knowing intellectually versus experiencing it. And so, there's also the, the striking thinness of the atmosphere, something that they see. And again, for most astronauts, the feeling that the earth itself is a whole system, and we're just a part of it. We need to think of ourselves as part of this organic system, if you will. And then there are other things that come out of it that is kind of a conclusion they draw. I mean, those are things they see, and then there are conclusions they

draw. And one of them is that we are really all in this together. Our fate is bound up with people that we may think are really different from them. We may have different religions, we may have different politics. But ultimately, we are connected. Totally connected. And not only with people, but with life. We're totally connected with life. And everything relates to everything else. And out of that, also, is the realization again. You could know that, too. I mean, you could say, I know that. I know we're all connected. I know our differences don't matter that much. But again, it's knowing it with the brain and not the heart. And so, the big, sort of, what would I call it, insight, about their experience is that it is an experience.[124]

The power of experience. I have had the privilege to spend hours with many different astronauts and listen to them speak about their experiences of space flight. If asked, they all mentioned the lack of borders. My friend, Dan Irwin, does like to point out the border between Mexico and Guatemala can be seen from space because of how the two countries have managed their forests differently, but barring that example, the earth really is this shared spaceship on which we are all traveling around the sun together.

A planet of life with humans not separated by nationality, gender, or that arbitrary construct of race—it is impossible to see the earth from space and see our differences. In fact, most of the astronauts I have spoken with have been deeply

124 Frank White, "The Overview Effect," interview by Gary Jordan, *Houston We Have a Podcast*, August 30, 2019. Accessed May 16, 2020.

touched by what unifies us most: that critical boundary between humanity and the vacuum of space, our precious atmosphere. Now, maybe because they have just rocketed through it, the experience of seeing that "thin blue line," all there is between us and certain death, leads astronauts to speak with reverence about it.

Carl Sagan helped us zoom even further out from low-Earth orbit, and from a distance of more than four billion miles. On February 14, 1990, Voyager One captured an image of Earth in which it is the tiniest little dot in the expanse of a small portion of our solar system. That little dot in the center of that sunbeam to the far right in Figure 3 is planet Earth. Our home. Our shared home. Our only home.

Figure 3. Credit: NASA/JPL

Sagan described it thus:

> *Look again at that dot. That's here. That's home. That's us. On it everyone you love, everyone you know, everyone you ever heard of, every human being who ever was, lived out their lives. The aggregate of our joy and suffering, thousands of confident religions, ideologies, and economic doctrines, every hunter and forager, every hero and coward, every creator and destroyer of civilization, every king and peasant, every young couple in love, every mother and father, hopeful child, inventor and explorer, every teacher of morals, every corrupt politician, every "superstar," every "supreme leader," every saint and sinner in the history of our species lived there—on a mote of dust suspended in a sunbeam.*[125]

Very few of us will actually ever travel to space and see that "thin blue line" in person and real time. It is incomprehensible any human could travel as far as Voyager did that Valentine's Day in 1990; yet, when I get present with that photo, it generates sincere, full-body awe. We humans are in need of some of that "reverential respect." Research from 2018 found:

> *Awe-prone individuals were rated as more humble by friends and reported greater humility across a two-week period, controlling for other positive emotions. Inducing awe led participants to present a more balanced view of their strengths and weaknesses to others and acknowledge, to a greater degree, the contribution of outside forces in their own personal accomplishments,*

---

125 Carl Sagan, *A Pale Blue Dot*, (Random House Publishing, 1994), 6.

compared with neutral and positive control conditions. Finally, an awe-inducing expansive view elicited greater reported humility than a neutral view.[126]

I believe we need more humility and greater recognition of the outside forces contributing to our own accomplishments if we have any hope of repairing society's systemic breakdowns and creating lasting systems change.

For our purposes here:

Systems are characterized by a set of actors and interactions that form a coherent whole, perform a specific function or functions, and have a boundary that sets the system apart from the rest of the world. Systems, simple or complex, are comprised of these four components:

- **Boundaries**: Parameters and limits that distinguish what's inside the system from what's outside the system (e.g., national, regional, sectoral)
- **Actors**: Formal and informal elements within a system (e.g., individuals, institutions–companies, research institutions, government bodies, etc.)
- **Linkages**: Simple and complex relationships and their consequences (e.g., interconnections and feedback loops)
- **Enabling Environment**: Interrelated conditions that impact actors within a specific boundary (e.g., infrastructure, policies, culture, history, etc.)[127]

---

126 Jennifer E. Stellar et al., "Awe and humility," *Journal of Personality and Social Psychology,* 114, no. 2 (2018).

127 Systems Leadership, "An introduction to the concepts, case studies, skills, and learning journeys that support Systems Leadership," researched by Global Knowledge Initiative. Accessed May 16, 2020.

Systems change is a "structural change to a system that is the result of forces in the enabling environment, between actors, and/or linkages."[128]

The scourge of COVID-19 has ripped off the scab of inequalities and highlighted the multitude of system breakdowns here in the United States that need repairing.

> In the last four weeks, as large sections of the global economy have shut down, more than thirty-three million Americans have filed for unemployment. People with jobs that aren't deemed essential, or that render telework impossible, are suddenly without work, and, in many cases, savings. According to the CEO of Feeding America, the pandemic is likely to leave an additional seventeen million Americans needing food assistance in the next six months. Recently, in Los Angeles, Pittsburgh, and Irving, Texas, people waited outside food pantries in lines that stretched miles. Tens of thousands of people who can't pay their bills have gone on rent strikes.
>
> The disaster has become so dire so quickly owing, in part, to the legacy of the 2008 financial crisis. Minimum wage, in real terms, is more than 30 percent lower than it was fifty years ago (since the 1980s, most of the benefits of America's growing economy have gone to the wealthy).

---

128 Ibid.

Meanwhile, housing costs have more than doubled since 2000. "When people say they live paycheck to paycheck, it's not that they're managing their money poorly," Sharon Parrott, a senior vice-president at the Center on Budget and Policy Priorities, told me. "Instead, their housing costs are taking up a disproportionate share of their incomes." The result is a slim margin of error: 40 percent of Americans don't have $400 cash to spare in an emergency, and would need to rely on credit cards or friends and family to come up with the money.[129]

COVID-19 has even highlighted the inequalities by geography.

> *Darnell Shields, executive director of the Chicago community group Austin Coming Together, said COVID-19's disparate impacts arise from food and housing instability, shaky neighborhood economies, and limited access to quality education and healthcare.*
>
> *USA TODAY took an exclusive look at how the pandemic has been felt in neighborhoods across the nation by collecting the ZIP code-level data from health departments in twelve states: Arizona, California, Florida, Illinois, Maryland, Michigan, Missouri, New York, Ohio, Pennsylvania, South Carolina, and Texas. COVID-19 case report summaries were assembled for more than 3,200 ZIP codes—about 10 percent of the nearly 33,000 in the US.*

---

129 Eliza Griswold, "How the Coronavirus is Killing the Middle Class," *The New Yorker,* May 14, 2020.

Case data were matched with census demographic data to show how infection rates differed in ZIP codes by race, income, and housing characteristics. The results paint a grim picture of COVID's devastation in places just miles or blocks from communities experiencing far less harm.

In the poorest neighborhoods, where median household income is less than $35,000, the COVID-19 infection rate was twice as high as in the nation's wealthiest ZIP codes, with income more than $75,000. Infection rates were five times higher in majority-minority ZIP codes than in ZIP codes with less than 10 percent non-white population. Of the top ten ZIP codes with ten or more cases—one in Florida, one in Michigan, the other eight in New York City—nine are areas where at least two-thirds of the residents are non-white. Five are areas where household income is below the national median of $60,293.[130]

As if income and racial disparities weren't enough, breakdowns in the healthcare system, our food systems, and the supply chains that support them both, our educational systems, and agreed-upon standards and sources for trusted data and information were all laid bare.

As I explore my own white fragility related to racism, thanks to the book with the same title by Robin DiAngelo, or see the earnings gap grow between classes, it could be easy to

---

130 Grace Hauck et al., "Coronavirus spares one neighborhood but ravages the next. Race and class spell the difference," *USA TODAY,* May 3, 2020. Accessed May 16, 2020.

get overwhelmed with sadness and frustration.[131] However, I can tap into that feeling of awe, and I can plug into the present moment and remember I have a choice, and therefore power. I must stay vigilant, stay in conversations with others, and continue to educate myself by integrating information from multiple sources and taking the time to reflect on what I learn. These practices help me to remain hopeful in light of the daily challenges faced by others and to remember to zoom out far enough to look at the system components so I can put my energy into creating structural change.

CHAPTER SUMMARY

Awe thrusts me into the moment while also connecting me to the expansiveness of the world around me. It can be useful as a quick fix for feeling the moment, but it is not an experience that can be maintained. The simple acts are the practices that can help support our efforts to create the changes to the systems that are broken and crumbling around us. For systems to change, we must keep up the practices. In our final chapter, we will explore ongoing practices to support our efforts.

---

131   Robin DiAngelo, *White Fragility*, (Boston: Beacon Press, June 26, 2018).

CHAPTER TWELVE

ONGOING PRACTICE

——

This shared journey is coming to end. The last chapter. Motivated by the systemic breakdowns I feel in the world today, I focused this book on simple acts we are already doing so they might be a pathway into the present moment. It is my hypothesis that we can most effectively make the decisions to fix the broken systems failing us when we take responsibilities to change them, and for that we must be in the present moment.

Accessing the present moment can give us the power of choices and therefore the chance to choose a different path. The concept of power has been implicit throughout and explicit at times during this conversation. Let's use Oxford's definition for the noun power:

1. The ability to do something or act in a particular way, especially as a faculty or quality.
2. The capacity or ability to direct or influence the behavior of others or the course of events.
3. Physical strength and force exerted by something or someone.

4. Energy that is produced by mechanical, electrical, or other means and used to operate a device.[132]

Before we remove definitions three and four (they don't meaningfully relate to the conversation we are in at the moment), let's once again recognize how messy verbal language can be. Oxford says when speaking about power, you can legitimately associate any of the above meanings, and those four are only for the noun version. If you mix in the verb version of power, you get two more!

Not only are there nuanced meanings according to Oxford, but I have my own experiences and meanings also associated with the word. I know of bad examples of definition two: Stalin and Hitler had the ability to direct the behavior of others (*definition two*) and because they had so much of that power, they altered the course of events (*definition two*) in a monstrous way. Greta Thunberg had the courage to act in a particular way (*definition one*) that ended up influencing the course of events in a significant way (*definition two*).

The complexity of definitions of common words is why the practice of listening for comprehension and understanding is so important. When we don't have a shared definition, we risk working at odds with others, or at least wasting effort because of misunderstandings. Some years ago, during a coaching session with my dear friend and talented coach, Jan Irene Miller, I was describing my care and concern for bringing a balance back into our relationship with the planet

---

132 *Lexico powered by Oxford.* s.v. "power," accessed May 25, 2020.

to enable a world full of possibilities and positive quality of life for everyone. She reflected on what I was sharing and proceeded to tell me what I really wanted was power. This assessment threw me off my center.

When she told me that, I immediately went to a negative Stalin/Hitler *definition two* type of power. That didn't feel good. This feeling was not what Jan Irene intended, and through the coaching process, she helped me to unpack her thoughts and my reaction, and eventually we navigated to a deeper understanding. Remember, too often in life there are not chances to or we don't take the time to explore our communication breakdowns with others, which leads to misunderstandings and more suffering when none was intended.

She was absolutely right about my desire for power. I needed to improve my *definition one* power, *ability to act in a particular way*, so I had *definition two* power, *to influence the course of events*. I saw breakdowns and problems in the world, and I felt them deeply. Yet in order to influence them, I needed new power. Systems change is hard work, and nearly impossible when the costs associated with the change are deemed higher than the rewards in that new future. This work is doubly hard when that new future can't be felt deeply enough to inspire action. The status quo proves too comfortable and familiar and we remain stuck.

But the status quo is not acceptable.

On May 30, 2020, SpaceX and NASA prepared for their second attempt to launch American astronauts to the International Space Station from US soil for the first time in nearly nine years. It was a day when our focus should have been on the best that humankind can achieve; however, on the same day, CNN headlines read, "Anger Boils over in More Than 30 Cities Leaving a Man Dead in Detroit and an Officer dead in Oakland after George Floyd's Death."[133]

People were angry and scared. Until we all address the root cause of racism in the United States, we will be doomed to continue to repeat these horrors. I have recently begun to confront the white privilege I have benefitted from my entire life. I sensed it, but never really explored it. This confrontation will be a lifelong journey for me. I will use the simple acts we have discussed to help support me on the way. These simple acts will give me the power to understand and change.

I invite you to take the power you have in the moment and consider making new choices. Start by educating and informing yourself to be more capable of creating the kind of change we need to make in the world so we don't continue to wake up with our cities on fire. For you listeners, check out the podcast series *1619*[134] and *Seeing White*.[135] I referenced *White Fragility* in the preceding chapter and encourage you to check it out, too, as racism all comes back to power.[136]

As John Biewen discovers in the third episode of *Seeing White*:

---

133 CNN, "Outrage Spills Across America," accessed May 30, 2020.

134 Nikole Hannah-Jones, "1619," August 23, 2019, produced by Annie Brown, Adizah Eghan, and Kelly Prime, podcast.

135 John Biewin, "Seeing White," *Scene On Radio*, February 15, 2017, podcast.

136 Robin DiAngelo, *White Fragility*, (Boston: Beacon Press, June 26, 2018).

Suzanne Plihcik and her colleagues with the Racial Equity Institute say, knowing this history, it's easier to see with clarity what racism is. They define it as social and institutional power, plus race prejudice. Or, put even more simply, a system of advantage based on race. "It is all about power. It revolves on power. It is not prejudice, it is not racial prejudice, it is not bigotry. It is power."[137]

How about the power of another idea: shareholder primacy. For the last forty years, the focus on maximizing shareholder value at the expense of everything else has taken a serious toll on our lives, society, and the natural world around us. As Rebecca Henderson describes the post-World War II era in her book *Reimagining Capitalism in a World on Fire*, this was not always the case.

This meant that for roughly thirty years after the war, in the developed world the state could be relied on to ensure that markets were reasonably competitive, that "externalities" such as pollution were properly priced or regulated, and that (nearly) everyone had the skills to participate in the market. Moreover, the experience of fighting the war created immense social cohesion. Investing in education and health, "doing the decent thing," and celebrating democracy seemed natural.[138]

---

137 John Biewin, "Made In America," *Seeing White*, *Scene On Radio*, Episode Three, March 16, 2017, podcast 33:39.

138 Rebecca Henderson, *Reimagining Capitalism in a World on Fire*. New York: PublicAffairs, 2020.

Just as the choice was made to focus solely on the shareholder at the expense of everything else, leaders are recognizing this cannot continue. Larry Fink, CEO of BlackRock, one of the world's leading asset management firms with nearly $6.5 trillion in assets under management as of March 31, 2020, wrote in his January 18, 2018 letter to shareholders:

> *Society is demanding that companies, both public and private, serve a social purpose. <u>To prosper over time, every company must not only deliver financial performance, but also show how it makes a positive contribution to society.</u> Companies must benefit all of their stakeholders, including shareholders, employees, customers, and the communities in which they operate.*[139]

Now we're talking, but what if we went even further? I recently had the pleasure of speaking with Michael Peck, the North American delegate to Mondragon (1999-2019) and co-founder of the 1worker1vote movement. A distinguished Naval Officer, public servant, executive, storyteller, and movement builder, Michael has dedicated his life to the idea of a prosperity for all. For those unfamiliar with Mondragon, here is his description from a talk he gave back in 2015:

> *A sixty-year-old experience, founded by a village priest....It started with collaboration. It started with soccer games because when people play sports together, they collaborate. He (the priest) opened a little school, and that school graduated five engineers who formed*

---

139 Larry Fink, Shareholder Letter, *BlackRock,* January 18, 2018.

a kerosene stove cooperative. Out of that came a move-
ment that today has 80,000 worker owners, $24 billion
in sales, our own bank, our own insurance company,
our own university, and the winner of the Financial
Times 2013 Boldness in Business Award, which is the
highest award the Financial Times gives.[140]

What I find so compelling about Mondragon is not its suc-
cess, although the origin story is inspiring, but how it han-
dled failure. Fagor, that first kerosene stove cooperative, had
grown into a $2 billion cooperative with a couple of thousand
worker owners supplying 37 percent of the domestic market
in Spain for stoves, kitchens, and bathrooms, but the 2008
financial crisis wiped out the market. Mondragon was in a
position and attempted to save Fagor with a $450 million
investment over five years, but in 2014 the company decided
any additional investment was not warranted.

What it did at that point is when it gets impressive. Mon-
dragon collectively voted for a 1.5 percent salary reduction
to support a fund that enabled the company to pay those
Fagor workers 85 percent of salaries and benefits. Within
eight months, they had cross-trained and found jobs for 1,500
workers. The company then found a buyer for Fagor that
committed to creating 700 jobs locally, so they were up 300
jobs after the devastation of the financial crisis. Peck shared
a couple of the lessons learned:

---

140 Michael Peck, "One Worker, One Vote and the Nationwide Union/Co-op
    Movement," June 15, 2015, video, 27:58.

When you own your own means of production, when you own your own decision-making processes, when you own your own supply chains, what does this allow you to do? It allows you to buy time. And when you buy time, it turns out that human beings are amazingly resourceful in terms of the solutions they can come up with. Necessity really is the madre and the padre of invention. The other thing it teaches us is that there is another way. In this country, what happens when companies fail? I've seen it with my own eyes, and so have you. The equipment gets bundled up and shipped off. The executives land with golden parachutes. The people are in the streets, a lot of them without benefits. The towns get hollowed out and we lose a generation of productivity. Really weak and increasingly weaker social platforms and mechanisms step in. Hardly anything comes up in its space. We spend years and years and years trying to realize what happened to these vital losses of our manufacturing DNA.[141]

During our recent conversation, Michael remains hopeful because more and more people are interested in the worker-owned business model. In fact, the first bipartisan employee-owner legislation in over twenty years, the Main Street Employee Ownership Act, was signed into law August 13, 2018. There are metrics that show the value and benefit from employee-owned business, and as he said, "They are more productive, more competitive, they retain their workforce, and more importantly, they are resilient." No wonder he remains hopeful, because we must have systems that are more resilient.

---

141 Ibid.

Oxford describes resilience as "the capacity to recover quickly from difficulties; toughness."[142] Given the findings in the mandated Fourth National Climate Assessment delivered to Congress and the president on November 23, 2018, we must become resilient because the effects of climate change are significant and pervasive. Communities, particularly coastal and indigenous communities, and people's health and well-being, are at greater risk. The overall economy, particularly agricultural productivity, tourism and recreation industries, and the nation's infrastructure, are also highlighted in the report because of their vulnerability to climate change. Here's what the report says about the systems we have become dependent on:

> *Climate change presents added risks to interconnected systems that are already exposed to a range of stressors such as aging and deteriorating infrastructure, land-use changes, and population growth. Extreme weather and climate-related impacts on one system can result in increased risks or failures in other critical systems, including water resources, food production and distribution, energy and transportation, public health, international trade, and national security. The full extent of climate change risks to interconnected systems, many of which span regional and national boundaries, is often greater than the sum of risks to individual sectors.*[143]

---

142 *Lexico powered by Oxford.* s.v. "resilience," accessed June 1, 2020.

143 U.S. Global Change Research Program, *Impacts, Risks, and Adaptation in the United States: Fourth National Climate Assessment, Volume II* ed. David Reidmiller, Christopher W. Avery, David R. Easterling, Kenneth E. Kunkel, Kristin Lewis, Thomas K. Maycock, and Brooke C. Stewart, Washington, DC, 2018.

We are moving into uncharted territory, and past experience will no longer serve as a sufficient guide as we try to navigate this uncertain future. However, I remain hopeful because communities are taking action. Experience on the front lines of climate change is proving more powerful than well-crafted sounds bites and messaging telling us it isn't real. I remain hopeful because Richard Moss and Kathy Jacobs have fought to create the Science for Climate Action Network, a commitment to support communities with appropriate and accurate science to assess their unique climate challenges and support them as they adapt.[144]

I remain hopeful because people like Stephen Burrington, executive director of Groundwork USA, are out fighting to make the world a better place. "Groundwork USA is the only network of local organizations devoted to transforming the natural and built environment of low-resource communities—a national enterprise with local roots, working at the intersection of the environment, equity, and civic engagement."[145]

Finally, I remain hopeful because we are all powerful people capable of making great change in our lives and the world. We have to begin from the present moment and in our bodies, where we have options and power. We have the power to make a difference! So count your next chew, bring consciousness to your next walk, really listen with your body in your next conversation, and find your next breath as you ask yourself, "for the sake of what?" Take back your power of the

---

144 SCAN: Science for Climate Action Network, accessed June 1, 2020.
145 "About us," Groundwork USA, accessed June 1, 2020.

moment, and as Mary Oliver says, "Determined to do the only thing you could do—determined to save the only life you could save." We've all got to start somewhere. I implore you to start with yourself, in this moment, in this body.

ACKNOWLEDGMENTS

———

Let's start at the beginning.

To my folks, thank you for creating such a loving environment full of opportunity and experience. I had the benefit of nurture and nature. To my bro, thank you for being an inspiration and helping me grow up.

To all my teachers who helped to shape my rough edges and polish my shine—particularly Vicki Piloseno, Dan Goldin, Jill Satterfield, Bob Dunham, Richard Strozzi-Heckler, the whole crew at the Hudson Institute of Coaching, and Doug Silsbee (rest in peace)—y'all really made this book possible by sharing your wisdom and knowledge and believing in me even when I didn't believe in myself sometimes. I'm merely sharing your wisdom and magic as best I can in the way I live my life.

Next up are the friends who have been instrumental in helping me find and refine these ideas: Dr. Rebecca Ocean, Jeff Hamaoui, James Parr, Jeremiah Palmer, Seema Patel, and Jan Irene Miller, thank you for the hours of conversation, insights, and pushes to become a better person.

Thank you to those who made this actual book possible. Amy Wilson, thank you for showing me the possibility. Eric Koester, thank you for creating the creative path and support network and not letting me stop when I had given up. Steven Jones, thank you for helping me get meaningfully on my path of exploring my white privilege. Michael Peck, thank you for your dedication to a new way of fair and equitable business and taking the time to share your energy and thoughts. Brian Bies and the entire New Degree Press publishing team, thank you for midwifing the process of turning a manuscript of ideas and stories into a beautiful book. Thank you especially, Kristy Carter, for staying by my side and encouraging me with your good cheer, spirit, and positive suggestions.

Thank you to all my beta readers who took the time to join me on this journey early, especially Barbara, Lori, Aunt Joyce, Morgane, Katie, Sara, Chris, Donna, and Nick. I owe a huge thanks to my awesome proofreaders, Rachel Dobkin, Vicki, and my momma. Any errors or shortcomings are a result of me not taking their advice.

And finally, to my wife Lady Anne and our pup Sirius, thank you for sacrificing all the hours over the last ten months and supporting me to get this book completed. It would not have been possible without your love and encouragement.

APPENDIX

———

INTRODUCTION

American Psychiatric Association. "Americans' Overall Level of Anxiety about Health, Safety and Finances Remain High." APA News Release. Accessed on April 10, 2020. https://www.psychiatry.org/newsroom/news-releases/americans-overall-level-of-anxiety-about-health-safety-and-finances-remain-high

Coleman-Jensen, Alisha, Matthew P. Rabbitt, Christian A. Gregory, Anita Singh. "Household Food Security in the United States in 2018." U.S. Department of Agriculture, Economic Research Service, *Economic Research Report* Number 270 (September 2019): Abstract

Pratt, Laura A., Deborah Brody, Qiuping Gu. "Antidepressant Use Among Persons Aged 12 and Over: United States, 2011–2014." *National Center for Health Statistics Data Brief* No. 283 (August 2017): Page 4.

TED. "Simon Sinek: How Great Leaders Inspire Action." March 10, 2014. Video, 17:58. https://www.ted.com/talks/simon_sinek_how_great_leaders_inspire_action?language=en

U.S. Census Bureau. "U.S. and World Population Clock."Accessed on April 10, 2020. https://www.census.gov/popclock/

U.S Department of Agriculture. "Why should we care about food waste?" Accessed on April 10, 2020. https://www.usda.gov/oce/foodwaste/faqs.htm

CHAPTER ONE
FOR THE SAKE OF WHAT

Collin, Richard E. "'We Choose to Go to the Moon', JFK and the Race for the Moon, 1960-1963" in John F. Kennedy History, Memory, Legacy: An Interdisciplinary Inquiry, edited by John Delane Williams, Robert G. Waite and Gregory S Gordon, Pages 167-78. University of North Dakota, UND Scholarly Commons. https://commons.und.edu/cgi/viewcontent.cgi?article=1002&context=oers

Editors of LIFE. "LIFE John F. Kennedy: The Legacy a 100-Year Commemorative Edition." *LIFE,* May 29, 2017.

Elliot, Derek W. "Space: The Final Frontier of the New Frontier" in Kennedy: The New Frontier Revisited, edited by Mark J. White, Chapter 6. NYU Press, 1998.

Kennedy, John F. "Special Message by the President on Urgent National Needs." Address to Congress, Washington, DC.May 25, 1961. https://www.jfklibrary.org/asset-viewer/archives/JFKPOF/034/JFKPOF-034-030

Lexico powered by Oxford. s.v. "practice(n.)." Accessed April 19, 2020. https://www.lexico.com/en/definition/practice

Oliver, Mary. "The Journey" in *Dream Work. New York: The Atlantic Monthly Press, 1986.*

Rossman, Robert J. and Mathew D. Duerden. *Designing Experiences.* Columbia University Press, 2019.

CHAPTER TWO
HOW WE GOT HERE

Cleveland Clinic. "Vital Signs."Accessed February 23, 2020. https://my.clevelandclinic.org/health/articles/10881-vital-signs

Constanza, Robert, Lisa J. Graumlich, and Will Steffen. "Sustainability or Collapse Lessons from Integrating the History of Humans and the Rest of Nature," in *Sustainability or Collapse?,* ed. Robert Constanza, Lisa J. Graumlich, and Will Steffen. Cambridge: The MIT Press, 2007.

Denning, Peter J. and Robert Dunham. *The Innovator's Way.* Cambridge: The MIT Press, 2010.

Gordon, Robert J. *The Rise and Fall of American Growth.* Princeton: Princeton University Press, 2016.

Hibbard, Kathy A., Paul J. Crutzen, Eric. F Lambin, Diana M. Liverman, Nathan J. Nantua, John R. McNeill, Bruno Messerli, and Will Steffen. "Group Report: Decadal-scale Interactions of Humans and the Environment," in *Sustainability or Collapse?,* ed. Robert Constanza, Lisa J. Graumlich, and Will Steffen. Cambridge: The MIT Press, 2007.

International Energy Agency. "SDG7: Data and Projections." *Flagship Report,* November 2019. Accessed February 23, 2020. https://www.iea.org/reports/sdg7-data-and-projections#

Landsberg, Steven. "A Brief History of Economic Time." *The Wall Street Journal,* June 9, 2007.

Lexico powered by Oxford. s.v. "quality of life(n.)." Accessed April 19, 2020. https://www.lexico.com/en/definition/quality_of_life

Mintz, Steven and Sara McNeil. Housework in Late 19th Century America. *Digital History.* Accessed February 23, 2020. http://www.digitalhistory.uh.edu/topic_display.cfm?tcid=93

Rieck, Thom. "10,000 steps a day: Too low? Too high?" *Mayo Clinic.* Accessed February 23, 2020.

TED. "Robert J. Gordon: The Death of Innovation, The End of Growth." April 23, 2013. Video, 12:11. https://www.ted.com/talks/robert_gordon_the_death_of_innovation_the_end_of_growth?language=en

United Nations. "Ending Poverty." Accessed February 23, 2020. https://www.un.org/en/sections/issues-depth/poverty/

United Nations. "Water, Sanitation and Hygiene." Accessed February 23, 2020. https://www.unwater.org/water-facts/water-sanitation-and-hygiene/

CHAPTER THREE
THE LIZARD BRAIN?

ACADEMIA SUPERIOR - Gesellschaft für Zukunftsforschung - Institute for Future Studies. "You are the product!" April 15, 2019, video, 6:19.https://www.youtube.com/watch?v=uGjofTSMIHg

Andrews, Edmund. "The Science Behind Cambridge Analytica: Does Psychological Profiling Work?" Stanford Graduate School of Business, April 12, 2018. Accessed February 27, 2020. https://www.gsb.stanford.edu/insights/science-behind-cambridge-analytica-does-psychological-profiling-work

Bureau of Transportation Statistics, United States Department of Transportation. "Transportation Fatalities by Mode." Accessed February 27, 2020. https://www.bts.gov/content/transportation-fatalities-mode

Centers for Disease Control and Prevention. "Mental Health in the Workplace." Accessed February 25, 2020. https://www.cdc.gov/workplacehealthpromotion/tools-resources/workplace-health/mental-health/index.html

Clear, James. "*Atomic Habits.*" (New York: Avery, 2018.

Fox, Maggie. "Major depression on the rise among everyone, new data shows." NBC News, May 11, 2018. Accessed February 25, 2020. https://www.nbcnews.com/health/health-news/major-depression-rise-among-everyone-new-data-shows-n873146

Health Resources and Services Administration. "The Loneliness Epidemic." Accessed February 25, 2020. https://www.hrsa.gov/enews/past-issues/2019/january-17/loneliness-epidemic

History.com Editors. "Flight 800 explodes over Long Island." Accessed February 27, 2020.https://www.history.com/this-day-in-history/flight-800-explodes-over-long-island

Houghton, Mick. "The Making Of... The Doors' Riders On The Storm." *Uncut.* February 2007 issue, Take 117. Accessed February 25, 2020. https://www.uncut.co.uk/features/the-making-of-the-doors-riders-on-the-storm-4035/

National Institute of Health Curriculum Supplement Series [Internet]. "Information About the Brain." Accessed February 25, 2020.

https://www.ncbi.nlm.nih.gov/books/NBK20367/

National Institute of Mental Health. "Mental Illness." Accessed February 25, 2020. https://www.nimh.nih.gov/health/statistics/mental-illness.shtml

National Institute of Mental Health. "Major Depression." Accessed February 25, 2020. https://www.nimh.nih.gov/health/statistics/major-depression.shtml

Reid, Jeffrey. "Pierre Salinger Syndrome and the TWA 800 Conspiracies." CNN, July 17, 2006. Accessed February 27, 2020. https://www.cnn.com/2006/US/07/12/twa.conspiracy/

Silsbee, Doug. "*Presence-Based Leadership: Complexity Practices for Clarity, Resilience, and Results That Matter.*" Asheville: Yes! Global Inc., 2018.

Troncale, Joseph. "Your Lizard Brain." *Psychology Today,* April 22, 2014. Accessed May 31, 2020. https://www.psychologytoday.com/us/blog/where-addiction-meets-your-brain/201404/your-lizard-brain

Tye, Larry. "*The Father of Spin.*" New York: Crown Publishers, 1998.

Zuckerman, Catherine. "The human brain, explained." National Geographic. October 15, 2009. Accessed February 25, 2020. https://www.nationalgeographic.com/science/health-and-human-body/human-body/brain/

CHAPTER FOUR
THE POWER OF NOW

Encyclopaedia Britannica Online. s.v. "René Descartes." accessed April 25, 2020. https://www.britannica.com/biography/Rene-Descartes

Evan Carmichael. "Oprah Winfrey's INSPIRING Story." November 18, 2017, video, 21:20. https://www.youtube.com/watch?v=Hv1q-doNPINA

Forbes. "Real Time Net Worth." accessed April 25, 2020. https://www.forbes.com/profile/oprah-winfrey/#424edcfe5745

Innovation Cities. "Eight Cambridge alumni who shook the world." *CNBC,* September 30, 2014. Accessed April 25, 2020. https://www.cnbc.com/2014/09/26/eight-cambridge-alumni-who-shook-the-world.html

Mancini, Flavia, Armando Bauleo, Jonathan Cole, Fausta Lui, Carlo A Porro, Patrick Haggard, and Gianni Domenico Iannetti. "Whole-Body Mapping of Spatial Acuity for Pain and Touch." *Annals of neurology*, 75(6), (Jun 2014): 917-24. https://doi.org/10.1002/ana.24179

Stanford Graduate School of Business. "Oprah Winfrey on Career, Life, and Leadership." April 28, 2014, video 1:04:03. https://www.youtube.com/watch?v=6DlrqeWrczs

Walker, Ether. "Eckhart Tolle: This man could change your life." *Independent,* June 21, 2008. Accessed April 25, 2020, https://www.independent.co.uk/news/people/profiles/eckhart-tolle-this-man-could-change-your-life-850872.html

CHAPTER FIVE
WHERE IS YOUR BREATH?

Hof, Wim. "Wim Hof Method." Accessed April 25, 2020. https://www.wimhofmethod.com/

Jester, Dylan J., Ellen K. Rozek, and Ryan A. McKelley. "Heart rate variability biofeedback: Implications for cognitive and psychiatric effects in older adults." *Aging & Mental Health* 23, 5 (2019): 574–580. https://doi.org/10.1080/13607863.2018.1432031

Lin, I. Mei, Sheng-Yu Fan, Cheng-Fan Yen, Yi-Chun Yeh, Tze-Chun Tang, Mei-Fung Huang, Tai-ling Liu, et al. "Heart rate variability biofeedback increased autonomic activation and improved symptoms of depression and insomnia among patients with major depression disorder." *Clinical Psychopharmacology and Neuroscience* 17, 2 (2019): 222–232. https://doi.org/10.9758/cpn.2019.17.2.222

Lin, Guiping, Qiuling Xiang, Xiaodong Fu, Shuzhen Wang, Sheng Wang, Sijuan Chen, Li Shao, et al. "Heart rate variability biofeedback decreases blood pressure in prehypertensive subjects by improving autonomic function and baroreflex." *Journal of Alternative and Complementary Medicine* 18, 2 (2012): 143–152. https://doi.org/10.1089/acm.2010.0607

Ma, Xiao, Zi-Qi Yue, Zhu-Qing Gong, Hong Zhang, Nai-Yue Duan, Yu-Tong Shi, Gao-Xia Wei and You-Fa-Li. "The Effect of Diaphragmatic Breathing on Attention, Negative Affect and Stress in Healthy Adults." *Frontiers in Psychology*, 8 (2017).

McKeown, Patrick. *The Oxygen Advantage.* New York: Harper Collins, 2015.

MedlinePlus. "Cerebral Hypoxia." *U.S. National Library of Medicine,* accessed April 25, 2020. https://medlineplus.gov/ency/article/001435.htm

Pagaduan, Jeffrey, Sam XS Wu, Tatiana Kameneva, and Elisabeth Lambert. "Acute effects of resonance frequency breathing on cardiovascular regulation." *Physiological Reports* 7, no. 2 (November 2019). https://doi.org/10.14814/phy2.14295

Satterfield, Jill. "Our Home of Practice." Accessed April 25, 2020. https://jillsatterfield.org/

Sawyer, Kathy. "NASA Confirms Second Liftoff for First American to Orbit Earth." *Washington Post,* January 17, 1998. https://www.washingtonpost.com/wp-srv/national/longterm/glenn/stories/confirms.htm

Steffen, Patrick R., Tara Austin, Andrea DeBarros, and Tracy Brown. "The Impact of Resonance Frequency Breathing on Measures of Heart Rate Variability, Blood Pressure, and Mood," *Frontiers in Public Health, 5 (2017). https://doi.org/10.3389/ fpubh.2017.00222*

Taghizadeh, Niloofar and Alireza Eslaminejad, and Mohammad Reza Raoufy. "Protective effect of heart rate variability biofeedback on stress-induced lung function impairment in asthma." *Respiratory Physiology & Neurobiology* 262 (April 2019): Pages 49-56. https://doi.org/10.1016/j.resp.2019.01.011

Zautra, Alex, Robert Fasman, Mary Davis and Arthur Craig. "The effects of slow breathing on affective responses to pain stimuli: An experimental study." *Pain, 149, 1 (2010): 12-18. 10.1016/j. pain.2009.10.001*

CHAPTER SIX
TRY LISTENING FOR A CHANGE

Czura, Christopher J., Mauricio Rosas-Ballina and Kevin J Tracey. "Cholinergic Regulation of Inflammation," in *Psychoneuroimmunology 4th edition,* ed. Robert Ader (Academic Press, 2007) https://www.sciencedirect.com/topics/neuroscience/vagus-nerve

Hayes, Seth A., Robert L. Rennaker and Michael P. Kilgard. "Targeting Plasticity with Vagus Nerve Stimulation to Treat Neurological Disease," *Progress in Brain Research* 207 (2013): 275-299. https://www.ncbi.nlm.nih.gov/pmc/articles/ PMC4615598/#!po=63.0435

Hirst, Barry H. "Secretin and the exposition of hormonal control." *Journal of Physiology* 560, part 2 (October 2015): 339. 10.1113/jphysiol.2004.073056

Institute for Generative Leadership. "A Unique Framework for Elevating Your Leadership and Coaching Impact." Accessed April 26, 2020. https://generateleadership.com/who-we-are/

Kaelberer, Melanie Maya, Kelly L. Buchanan, Marguerita E. Klein, Bradley B. Barth, Marcia M. Montoya, Xiling Shen, and Diego V. Bohorquez. "A gut-brain neural circuit for nutrient sensory transduction." *Science* 361, 6408 (September 18). https://science.sciencemag.org/content/361/6408/eaat5236

Lexico powered by Oxford. s.v. "sough." Accessed April 26, 2020. https://www.lexico.com/en/definition/sough

Schmidt, Norman B., J. Anthony Ritchey, Michael J. Zvolensky and Jon K. Maner. "Exploring Human Freeze Responses to a Threat Stressor." *Journal of Behavior Therapy and Experimental Psychiatry* 39, 3 (September 2008): 292-304. https://doi.org/10.1016/j.jbtep.2007.08.002

Schwartz, Michael W., Stephen C. Woods, Daniel Porte Jr., Randy J. Seeley and Denis G. Baskin. "Central nervous system control of food intake," *Nature* 404 (2000): 661-671. https://doi.org/10.1038/35007534

Underwood, Emily. "Your gut is directly connected to your brain, by a newly discovered neuron circuit." *Science Magazine,* September 20, 2018. https://www.sciencemag.org/news/2018/09/your-gut-directly-connected-your-brain-newly-discovered-neuron-circuit#

CHAPTER SEVEN
CHEW YOUR FOOD

Barnard, Neal. Physicians Committee for Responsible Medicine. Accessed April 25, 2020. https://www.pcrm.org/yourbodyin-balance

Encyclopaedia Britannica Online. s.v. "Ivan Pavlov." accessed April 25, 2020. https://www.britannica.com/biography/Ivan-Pavlov

Institute for Integrative Nutrition. "About Us." Accessed April 25, 2020. https://www.integrativenutrition.com/about-us

Nestle, Marion. *FOOD POLITICS: HOW THE FOOD INDUSTRY INFLUENCES NUTRITION AND HEALTH.* University of California Press: 2003.

AM Pederson, A Bardow, S Beier Jensen, and B Nauntofte. "Saliva and gastrointestinal functions of taste, mastication, swallowing and digestion." *Oral Diseases* 8, 3 (May 2020). https://doi.org/10.1034/j.1601-0825.2002.02851.x

Stanchich, Lino. *Power Eating Program.* Asheville: Healthy Products, Inc., 1989.

CHAPTER EIGHT
WALKING

Guinness World Records. "Fastest journey of the Pan-American highway on foot." Accessed April 26, 2020. https://www.guinnessworldrecords.com/world-records/fastest-journey-on-foot-pan-american-highway

Jabr, Ferris. "Why Walking Helps Us Think." *New Yorker*, September 3, 2014. https://www.newyorker.com/tech/annals-of-technology/walking-helps-us-think

Masao, Fidelis T, Elgidius B Ichumbaki, Mario Cherin, Angelo Barili, Giovanni Boschian, David A Iurino, Sofia Menconero et al. "New footprints from Laetoli (Tanzania) provide evidence for marked body size variation in early hominins." *eLife* 5 (December 2016). 10.7554/eLife.19568

Matthews, Amy. Embodied Asana. Accessed April 26, 2020. https://embodiedasana.com/about-amy/

McLaughlin, Rose. *Meegan - A Short Documentary.* February 15, 2016. Video, 5:20. https://www.youtube.com/watch?v=5zD-SvP5nQe0

PBS. "Laetoli Footprints." Evolution Library. Accessed April 26, 2020. https://www.pbs.org/wgbh/evolution/library/07/1/l_071_03.html

Smithsonian National Museum of Natural History. "Laetoli Footprint Trails" What does it mean to be human? Accessed April 26, 2020. http://humanorigins.si.edu/evidence/behavior/footprints/laetoli-footprint-trails

Stillman, Jessica. "The Simple Trick Great Thinkers From Charles Darwin to Steve Jobs Used to Be More Creative." *Inc.,* Accessed April 26, 2020. https://www.inc.com/jessica-stillman/steve-jobs-swore-by-walking-meetings-heres-science-of-why-they-re-awesome-how-to-do-them-right.html

Ward, Carol. "Unraveling the Mystery of Human Bipedality." Interview by Tom Garlinghouse, *Sapiens* May 29, 2019. https://www.sapiens.org/archaeology/human-bipedality/

CHAPTER NINE
I SMELL THAT

Alexander, Lloyd. *The Book of Three.* New York: Henry Holt and Company, 1964.

Grand View Research. Perfume Market Size, Share & Trends Analysis Report By Product (Mass, Premium), By End User (Men, Women), By Distribution Channel (Offline, Online), By Region, And Segment Forecasts, 2019 - 2025. Jun 2019. https://www.grandviewresearch.com/industry-analysis/perfume-market

Holland, Alisha C. and Elizabeth A. Kensinger. "Emotion and Autobiographical Memory." *Physics of Life Review,* 7, no. 1 (Mar 2010): 89. 10.1016/j.plrev.2010.01.006

Kaufman, David Myland. *Clinical Neurology for Psychiatrists, Chapter 4 Cranial Nerve Impairments.* Elsevier, 2007. https://www.sciencedirect.com/science/article/pii/B9781416030744100049?via%3Dihub

Kiechle, Melanie. "The Smell Detectives." *Science History Institute,* June 19, 2011. Accessed April 26, 2020. https://www.sciencehistory.org/distillations/the-smell-detectives

Larsson, Maria, Johan Willander, Kristina Karlsson and Artin Arshamian, "Olfactory LOVER: behavioral and neural correlates of autobiographical odor memory." *Frontiers in Psychology,* 5, no. 312. April 11, 2014. 10.3389/fpsyg.2014.00312

Moore, Malcom. "Eau de BC: the oldest perfume in the world." *The Telegraph,* March 21, 2007. https://www.telegraph.co.uk/news/worldnews/1546277/Eau-de-BC-the-oldest-perfume-in-the-world.html

Pettit, Don. "The Smell of Space." Expedition Six Space Chronicles #4. https://spaceflight.nasa.gov/station/crew/exp6/spacechronicles4.html

Robbins, Tom. *Jitterbug Perfume.* New York: Bantam Books, 1990.

Secundo, Lavi, Kobi Snitz, Kineret Weissler, Liron Pinchover, Yehuda Shoenfeld, Ron Loewenthal, Nancy Agmon-Levin, Idan Frumin, Dana Bar-Zvi, Sagit Shushan, and Noam Sobel. "Individual olfactory perception reveals meaningful nonolfactory genetic information," *Proceedings of the National Academy of Science.* 112, no. 28. Jul 2015. https://doi.org/10.1073/pnas.1424826112

Thorpe, JR. "The Strange History Of Perfume, From Ancient Roman Foot Fragrance To Napoleon's Cologne." *Bustle,* July 31, 2015. https://www.bustle.com/articles/101182-the-strange-history-of-perfume-from-ancient-roman-foot-fragrance-to-napoleons-cologne

University of California - San Diego. "Loss of smell and taste validated as COVID-19 symptoms in patients with high recovery rate: Study suggests clinicians should include sensory impairment as standard screening measure." ScienceDaily, April 13, 2020. Accessed May 10, 2020. www.sciencedaily.com/releases/2020/04/200413132809.htm

CHAPTER TEN
INFORMAL PRACTICE

Beveridge, Charles. "Frederick Law Olmsted Sr." National Association for Olmsted Parks. Accessed May 24, 2020. https://www.olmsted.org/the-olmsted-legacy/frederick-law-olmsted-sr

Biltmore Estate. "Grounds and Gardens." Accessed May 24, 2020. https://www.biltmore.com/visit/biltmore-estate/gardens-grounds/

Lin, Wei, Qibing Chen, Mingyan Jiang, Jinying Tao, Zongfang Liu, Xiaoxia Zhang, Linjia Wu, Shan Xu, Yushan Kang, and Qiuyuan Zeng. "Sitting or Walking? Analyzing the Neural Emotional Indicators of Urban Green Space Behavior with Mobile EEG." *Journal of Urban Health* 97 (2020): 191–203. https://doi.org/10.1007/s11524-019-00407-8

Rossman, Robert J. and Mathew D. Duerden. *Designing Experiences.* Columbia University Press, 2019.

White, Matthew P, Nicola L Yeo, Peeter Vassiljev, Rikard Lundstedt, Mattias Wallergard, Marina Albin, and Mare Lohmus. "A prescription for "nature" – the potential of using virtual nature in therapeutics." *Neuropsychiatric Disease and Treatment* 14 (2018): 3001-3013. https://doi.org/10.2147/NDT.S179038

World Health Organization. Global Health Observatory. "Urban Population Growth." Accessed May 24, 2020. https://www.who.int/gho/urban_health/situation_trends/urban_population_growth_text/en/

CHAPTER ELEVEN
THE OVERVIEW EFFECT

DiAngelo, Robin. *White Fragility.* Boston: Beacon Press, June 26, 2018.

Griswold, Eliza. "How the Coronavirus is Killing the Middle Class." *The New Yorker,* May 14, 2020.

Hauck, Grace, Mark Nichols, MiriamI Marini and Andrew Pantazi. "Coronavirus spares one neighborhood but ravages the next. Race and class spell the difference." *USA Today,* May 3, 2020.

Lexico powered by Oxford. s.v. "awe." Accessed May 16, 2020. https://www.lexico.com/en/definition/awe

Sagan, Carl. *A Pale Blue Dot.* Random House Publishing, 1994.

Stellar, Jennifer E., Amie Gordon, Craig L. Anderson, Paul K. Piff, Galen D. McNeil, and Dacher Keltner. "Awe and humility." *Journal of Personality and Social Psychology,* 114, no. 2 (2018). https://doi.org/10.1037/pspi0000109

Systems Leadership. "An introduction to the concepts, case studies, skills, and learning journeys that support Systems Leadership." Researched by Global Knowledge Initiative. Accessed May 16, 2020. http://globalknowledgeinitiative.org/wp-content/uploads/2018/02/18.01.31-GKI-Systems-Leadership-Brief_USAID-FINAL.pdf

White, Frank. "The Overview Effect." Interview by Gary Johnson, *Houston We Have a Podcast.* August 30, 2019. https://www.nasa.gov/johnson/HWHAP/the-overview-effect

CHAPTER TWELVE
ONGOING PRACTICE

Biewin, John. "Seeing White," *Scene On Radio*, February 15, 2017. Podcast. https://www.sceneonradio.org/seeing-white/

Biewin, John. "Made In America." *Seeing White, Scene On Radio,* Episode Three. March 16, 2017. Podcast, 33:39. https://www.sceneonradio.org/episode-33-made-in-america-seeing-white-part-3/

CNN. "Outrage Spills Across America." Accessed May 30, 2020. https://www.cnn.com/

DiAngelo, Robin. *White Fragility.* Boston: Beacon Press, June 26, 2018.

Fink, Larry. Shareholder Letter. *BlackRock,* January 18, 2018. https://www.nytimes.com/interactive/2018/01/16/business/dealbook/document-BlackRock-s-Laurence-Fink-Urges-C-E-O-s-to-Focus.html?dlbk

Groundwork USA. "About us." Accessed June 1, 2020. https://groundworkusa.org/about-us/

Hannah-Jones, Nikole. "1619." August 23, 2019. Produced by Annie Brown, Adizah Eghan, and Kelly Prime. Podcast. https://www.nytimes.com/2019/08/23/podcasts/1619-slavery-anniversary.html

Henderson, Rebecca. *Reimagining Capitalism in a World on Fire.* New York: PublicAffairs, 2020), 24

Lexico powered by Oxford. s.v. "power." Accessed May 25, 2020. https://www.lexico.com/en/definition/power

Lexico powered by Oxford. s.v. "resilience." Accessed June 1, 2020. https://www.lexico.com/en/definition/resilience

Peck,Michael. "One Worker, One Vote and the Nationwide Union/Co-op Movement." June 15, 2015. Video, 27:58. https://www.youtube.com/watch?v=_6x85Xy9KN8

SCAN: Science for Climate Action Network. Accessed June 1, 2020. https://www.climateassessment.org/

U.S. Global Change Research Program. *Impacts, Risks, and Adaptation in the United States: Fourth National Climate Assessment, Volume II.* Ed. David Reidmiller, Christopher W. Avery, David R. Easterling, Kenneth E. Kunkel, Kristin Lewis, Thomas K. Maycock, and Brooke C. Stewart. Washington, DC, 2018. https://nca2018.globalchange.gov/#sf-1

Made in the USA
Columbia, SC
16 August 2020